bake it

DK

DK | Penguin Random House

Senior editor Carrie Love
Project art editor Polly Appleton

Project art editors Jaileen Kaur, Nehal Verma
Senior designer Nidhi Mehra
Project editor Radhika Haswani
Editorial assistant Becky Walsh
DTP designer Neeraj Bhatia
Illustrator Rachael Hare
Home economist Denise Smart
Pre-production senior producer Nikoleta Parasaki
Producer John Casey
Jacket designer Elle Ward
Jacket co-ordinator Issy Walsh
Project picture researcher Sakshi Saluja
Delhi team head Malavika Talukder
Managing editors Penny Smith, Monica Saigal
Managing art editors Mabel Chan, Romi Chakraborty
Creative director Helen Senior
Publishing director Sarah Larter

This edition published in 2019 by
Dorling Kindersley Limited
DK, One Embassy Gardens, 8 Viaduct Gardens,
London, SW11 7BW

Material used in this book was previously published in:
The Cook's Book (2005),
The Children's Baking Book (2009),
Cook Step by Step (2010),
Step-by-Step Baking (2011),
A Little Course in Baking (2013),
Step-by-Step Cake Decorating (2013),
Kids' Birthday Cakes Step by Step (2014),
Step-by-Step Desserts (2015),
Eat Your Greens (2016),
Cooking Step by Step (2018)

The authorised representative in the EEA is
Dorling Kindersley Verlag GmbH. Arnulfstr. 124,
80636 Munich, Germany

Copyright © 2019 Dorling Kindersley Limited
A Penguin Random House Company
10 9 8 7 6 5
008–314399–Oct/2019

A CIP catalogue record for this book
is available from the British Library.
ISBN: 978-0-2413-8264-6

Printed and bound in China

For the curious
www.dk.com

MIX
Paper from
responsible sources
FSC™ C018179

This book was made with Forest
Stewardship Council™ certified
paper – one small step in DK's
commitment to a sustainable
future. For more information go to
www.dk.com/our-green-pledge

Contents

Creative cakes, cupcakes, and muffins

No-bakes

Kitchen rules

Baking is meant to be fun and a little bit messy, but you still need to keep safety and cleanliness in mind. Follow instructions carefully, gather everything together, and read through these rules and tips before you begin.

Ingredients

- Make sure you have all your ingredients laid out before you start to make a recipe. You'll probably have most ingredients in your kitchen already, but some you will need to buy.

- Always use the type of flour specified in a recipe – strong, plain, or self-raising.

- Use medium-sized eggs unless stated otherwise.

Preheating the oven

Follow the temperature instructions within each recipe.

Special equipment

Keep an eye out for recipes that require special equipment. Buy or borrow items in advance if you don't own them.

Weights and measurements

Carefully weigh out the ingredients before you start a recipe. Use measuring spoons, weighing scales, and a measuring jug as necessary. Below are the abbreviations and full names for the measurements used in this book.

Metric	Imperial measures	Spoon measures
g = gram	oz = ounce	tsp = teaspoon
ml = millilitre	lb = pound	tbsp = tablespoon
	fl oz = fluid ounce	

Level rating

Each recipe has a level rating to let you know how easy it will be to make.

 Super simple

 Nice and easy

 A bit tricky

 Super-skilled

How long?

This tells you how many minutes and hours a recipe will take to prepare, bake, chill, or freeze. Remember though that preparation times might take a little longer if it's the first time you're making a recipe.

How many?

This lists the amount of portions a recipe makes. Remember to be treat wise and don't go overboard by eating more than one portion.

Top tip

You'll find extra bits of advice in the Top tips throughout the book.

Kitchen safety

Be very careful...

- Around hot ovens, and gas or electric cookers, making sure you know whether the oven or cooker is on, and protecting your hands when touching or lifting anything hot from or on or into it. Oven gloves are your friend here!

- Handling hot liquids or hot pans, watching carefully for spillages, and protecting your hands (oven gloves or a tea towel) when moving or holding hot items. Tell an adult immediately if you get a burn.

- Handling anything sharp such as knives or a grater.

- Using power tools such as blenders, food processors, mixers, microwaves. Check if they're on, and don't put your hands near the moving parts until you have switched them off at the socket.

IF IN DOUBT ask an **ADULT** to help, especially when you're unsure about anything.

TRY THIS

Look out for these variation suggestion boxes. You can sometimes alter the ingredients to create a slightly different version of a recipe.

Kitchen hygiene

When you're in the kitchen, follow these important rules to keep the germs in check.

- Always wash your hands before you start any recipe.

- Wash all fruit and vegetables.

- Use separate chopping boards for meat and vegetables. Use hot, soapy water to clean the boards after using them.

- Store raw and cooked food separately.

- Keep meat in the fridge until you need it and always take care to cook it properly.

- Wash your hands after handling raw eggs or raw meat.

- Always check the use-by date on all ingredients.

- Keep your cooking area clean and have a cloth handy to mop up any spillages.

Getting started

1 Read a recipe all the way through before you start.

2 Wash your hands, put on an apron, and tie back your hair.

3 Make sure you have all the ingredients and equipment to hand before you begin cooking.

Equipment

Here is a handy guide for the baking equipment used throughout this book. Always follow the guidelines in the recipes for a particular size tin, tray, sheet, or dish as the ingredients may not fit otherwise.

Kitchen scissors Paintbrushes Peelers Garlic crusher

Wooden spoons Whisk Basting brush Large metal spoon Serrated knife Sharp knife Pizza cutter Table knife Fork Spoons Sugar thermometer

Baking trays and tins Pizza tray Square cake tin Loaf tin

Paper cake cases 12-hole cupcake tin Sandwich cake tin Paper muffin cases

Wire rack Cutting boards Mini cake tin about 6.5 x 2.5cm (2.5 x 1in) Non-stick muffin tin

Large bowl Metal bowl Glass bowls Small bowls Milk pan

Measuring spoons

Measuring cups

Glass jugs

Food processor

Food blender

Electric whisk

Injector

Plunger cutters

Piping bag and nozzles

Ramekin

Lemon juicer

Cookie cutters

Pastry cutter

Sieve

Slotted spoon

Palette knife

Spatula

Plastic spatula

Ice cream scoop

Fluted wheel

Zester

Measuring jug

Rolling pin

Baking parchment

Plastic container

Baking beans

Colander

Water spray

Grater

Foil

Cling film

10cm (4in) loose-bottomed tart tin

Oven dish

Pie dish

Metal flan dish

Skewers

Icing smoother

Frying pan

A selection of saucepans, including a heavy-based one

Turntable

Icing scrapers

Baking techniques

To get cakes to rise, make light meringue, and perfect your pastry and biscuits, there are certain techniques in baking that you'll need to master. Once you know what's what you'll be a baking expert!

Fold

1 Use a spatula to gently mix while keeping the air in the mixture.

2 Go around the edge of the bowl and then "cut" across the middle, lifting as you go.

Sift

Shaking flour or icing sugar through a sieve gets rid of lumps and adds air.

Separate an egg

1 To break the shell, tap the egg on the side of the bowl and open it up.

2 Transfer the yolk from one shell to the other; put the yolk in another bowl.

Whisk egg whites

1 In a spotlessly clean bowl, mix a lot of air into the egg whites, using an electric whisk.

2 The egg whites should be stiff. If you overwhisk, they will collapse, as shown here.

Knead

1 Use the heel of your hand to push the dough away from you.

2 Fold the squashed end of dough over and turn the whole lot round.

3 Repeat the squashing, folding, and turning motions until the dough is silky soft and smooth. Now the dough is ready to prove (get bigger).

Knock back

To "knock back" the dough, lightly punch it. This knocks out any large air bubbles.

Roll out

On a floured surface, roll a rolling pin over the dough to flatten it out.

Cream

1 When mixing butter and sugar together, use butter that's been left to soften at room temperature. Cut the butter into pieces first.

2 Using an electric whisk or a wooden spoon, beat the butter and sugar together until it's paler in colour, light, and fluffy.

Beat

Make a smooth, airy mixture by stirring quickly with a wooden spoon.

Rub in

1 Many recipes mix fat (diced butter or lard) and flour using this method.

2 Using your fingertips, pick up the mixture, break up the lumps, and let it fall.

3 Keep rubbing your thumb along your fingertips. To check you've got rid of all the lumps, shake the bowl. Any lumps will pop up to the surface.

Shortcrust pastry

This pastry is used to line savoury and sweet tarts and pies, and it doesn't puff up on baking. For light pastry, the key is to keep everything cool, including your hands, and not to overwork the dough.

1 It is important to use only your fingertips when rubbing the butter into the flour as this minimizes contact with body heat, which would melt the butter and make the pastry heavy and greasy.

2 Mix in enough cold water to bind the dough together. Too much water will make the pastry steam on baking, which will make it fragile and shrink back. The dough should be soft, but not sticky once fully mixed.

3 Shape the dough into a ball without overworking it, which could make the pastry greasy and tough. Shortcrust pastry must be chilled in a fridge for at least 30 minutes before shaping it into a tin to bake.

Grease a tin

Use baking parchment to spread a thin layer of butter all over the inside of the tin.

Line a tin

1 Draw around the tin. Cut out the shape, leaving enough extra parchment to cover the sides of the tin.

2 Position the parchment in the tin so it covers the base and the sides. Cut off the overhang.

Choux pastry

Choux pastry is a very light and airy pastry that is used for baking profiteroles. By beating enough air into the soft, doughy mixture you will guarantee crisp and light pastry that will rise beautifully as it bakes.

1 The traditional technique for beating flour into melted butter and water is called "shooting" the flour. Beat the mixture vigorously, but stop when it forms a ball of soft dough that comes away from the sides of the pan.

2 Using a wooden spoon, beat the eggs into the mixture a little at a time. Adding the eggs one at a time makes it easier to mix them in and with each beating you add more air. The dough should now be soft enough to pipe.

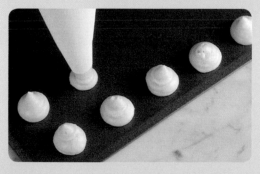

3 Fit a piping bag with a plain nozzle and fill it with the dough. With one hand at the top of your piping bag and one at the bottom, squeeze the dough out from the top into even rounds, leaving space in between each one.

Icing

Buttercream is the perfect covering for cakes and cupcakes, royal icing is great for piping work as it hardens quickly, and traditional royal icing is ideal for attaching cake decorations. Here are the best methods for making them.

Basic vanilla buttercream icing

Ingredients

300g (10oz) unsalted butter
2 tsp vanilla extract
600g (1lb 5oz) icing sugar
colouring paste (optional)

1 Cream the butter and vanilla together with an electric whisk. Add the icing sugar, beating well. Beat in 1–2 teaspoons of hot water, until the icing is light and fluffy.

2 Transfer to a bowl and add colouring paste, a little at a time, until you get the right colour.

Royal icing for piping

Ingredients

3 egg whites
1 tsp lemon juice, plus extra if needed
700g (1¾lb) icing sugar, sifted
colouring paste (optional)

1 Whisk the egg whites in a large bowl. Stir in the lemon juice. Gradually add the icing sugar.

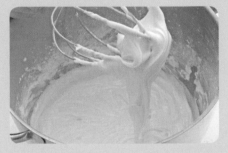

2 Continue to beat until the icing has a smooth, toothpaste-like consistency.

Traditional royal icing

Ingredients

3 egg whites
700g (1¾lb) icing sugar, sifted, plus extra if needed
1 tsp lemon juice
2 tsp glycerine

1 Whisk the egg whites in a large bowl until they are foamy. Add the icing sugar a spoonful at a time.

2 Stir in the lemon juice and glycerine, and beat until stiff, thick, and peaks begin to form.

Piping

Piping icing onto a cake takes a steady hand, so don't worry if you don't master it straight away. It's all about getting lots of practise. Here are tips for filling a piping bag and applying the icing to a baked cake.

Filling a piping bag

1 Fit the nozzle to the piping bag and place it upright in a tall glass. Spoon in the buttercream icing.

2 Remove the bag from the glass and squeeze the icing towards the nozzle. Lay the bag on a surface and press towards the nozzle, using a scraper, if desired.

3 Twist the bag at the top, to make sure that the icing is tightly sealed in. Hold the bag in one hand and steady the nozzle with your other hand. Squeeze the top of the bag (just below the twist) to get the icing to come out.

Basic royal icing piping

1 Fill the piping bag with royal icing. Hold the bag in your right hand (or left, if you are left-handed), between your thumb and first two fingers. Hold the bag steady with your other hand. When the nozzle touches the surface of the cake, gently squeeze the icing out.

2 Use even pressure as too little pressure will produce scrawny lines, while too much will make piping difficult to control. Let the icing catch the surface and then gently lift the nozzle away from the surface, letting the icing fall. At the end of the line, stop the pressure and lift the nozzle away.

Filling and layering cakes

Showstopper cakes often have several layers. Follow the steps below for layering a cake with icing to build several levels. Before you ice a cake, do a crumb coat layer first as this prevents bits coming off when you ice the cake.

Testing a cake is cooked

Insert a skewer into the middle of the cake. If it comes out clean, the cake is cooked.

Levelling a cake

Carefully remove the dome from the top of the cake using a serrated knife.

Layering and crumb coating a cake

1 Put the board on a turntable, dot with a blob of icing, and centre the base layer on top, levelled side up. Pipe icing around the edge.

2 Using a spoon, put a large dollop of icing in the centre and spread to the edges with a palette knife, until smooth.

3 Put the next layer on, levelled side down. To build the cake higher, repeat, with the levelled sides facing each other.

4 To crumb caot the cake, start at the top, and swirl the icing over the surface as you turn it around on the turntable.

5 Spread the icing around the sides until evenly covered. A few crumbs may be embedded in the icing; this is normal.

6 Refrigerate or allow to dry – this can take up to two hours. Add the final layer of icing.

Icing a cake

This method works best of all with buttercream icing, although you could use ganache or whipped cream instead. Using a palette knife and scraper, smooth your cake to an absolutely perfect finish.

1 With the cake on the turntable, put a large dollop of buttercream icing onto the centre of the cake.

2 Using a palette knife, swirl and smooth the icing, spreading it outwards and over the sides as you go.

3 Turn the cake as you spread the icing down and around the sides, to cover it evenly. When smooth, let the cake set for 10 minutes, and then repeat.

4 Put the blade of a palette knife in a jug of boiling water. When it is hot, dry it, and run it around the sides, turning the cake around with the flat surface of the knife against the icing. Repeat until the icing is smooth.

5 Make the top smooth with a hot knife, turning the cake with the flat surface of the knife against the icing. Move from one side of the cake to the other. Allow the cake to set for 15 minutes.

6 Use a scraper to smooth the icing all the way around the cake.

Piping cupcakes

Put a jam or icing filling into your cupcakes. Then, for a professional-looking finish, pipe buttercream icing into a swirl. Alternatively, try out different nozzles for stars, shells, or a variety of effects and textures. To finish, sprinkle your favourite toppings over the piped icing.

1 If you have thin, smooth icing or jam, you can use a plain round nozzle (shown above) or an injector nozzle on a piping bag. Attach the nozzle, load the bag with filling, and push it into the centre of the cupcake. Gently press on the bag until the icing fills the hole you've just made.

2 To ice the top of the cupcake, hold the nozzle 1cm (½in) straight above the cupcake and pipe from the outside edge inwards, in a spiral. Apply pressure so that an even amount comes out.

3 Build several layers of icing in a spiral movement, making each layer slightly smaller as you go.

4 Release the pressure to end the spiral at the centre of the cupcake. Decorate with sprinkles or edible glitter.

Covering a cake

Add an outer layer of rolled out fondant or marzipan to cakes for an extra special finish. Flatten out the air bubbles as you cover a cake with this clever technique using a smoother. The thickness of the fondant or marzipan should only ever be 4–5mm (⅙–¼in), so it doesn't overpower the flavours in the cake.

1 Dust a surface with icing sugar. Knead and roll the fondant or marzipan into a circle that can cover the cake with 5cm (2in) extra overhang.

2 Unroll the fondant or marzipan sheet onto the cake and smooth it across the top with a smoother, easing it down with your hands.

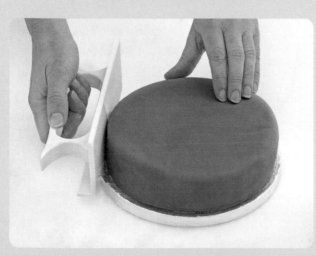

3 Trim off the excess fondant or marzipan. Press the smoother evenly over the top of the cake and then run it down and around the sides of the cake, until perfectly smooth. To get a sharp edge at the top of the cake, you can use two smoothers at the same time, one on the top and the other on the sides, pressing them together at the edge.

TRY THIS

For mini cakes, the fondant should be 2–3mm (1⁄16–⅛in) thick. For cupcakes, cut out circles of fondant to sit on top of the cupcakes.

Making meringues

Meringues are made by whisking lots of air into egg whites, then whisking in sugar. The mixture is then shaped and baked slowly on a low heat so that the moisture in the mixture evaporates, leaving you with crisp meringues that are light as air.

Use a clean bowl, with no grease.

Scrape the sides of the bowl with a spatula.

1 For a light and crisp meringue, you must whisk egg whites vigorously using an electric whisk. This stretches the protein in the egg whites, which helps to incorporate air into the mix and, as a result, increases the volume in the egg whites.

2 Using an electric whisk, beat in a spoonful of sugar at a time; any quicker and you may deflate the mixture. The whisked egg whites will become smoother and glossier with every addition of sugar.

Whisk until peaks form.

3 Take care to dissolve the sugar into the egg whites by whisking very well after each addition. The mixture will no longer feel grainy when the sugar has fully dissolved.

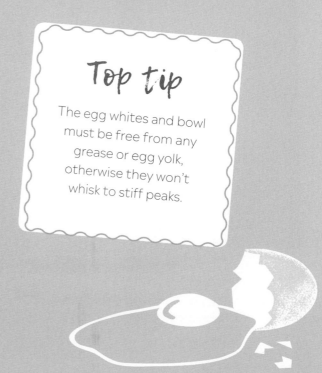

Top tip

The egg whites and bowl must be free from any grease or egg yolk, otherwise they won't whisk to stiff peaks.

Melting chocolate

Whether you want to cover a cake in chocolate, use moulds to create chocolate decorations, or make decorative curls, you must melt and temper chocolate. Tempering chocolate improves its consistency before you use it and gives a hard and glossy finish once it cools down.

Level rating

How long?
10 mins prep,
10 mins cooking

How many?
500g (1lb 2oz), enough to cover a cake or fill 3 large moulds

Ingredients

500g (1lb 2oz) good-quality milk, dark, or white chocolate

Special equipment
sugar thermometer

In a microwave

1 Break the chocolate into squares, put it in a microwavable bowl, and heat on full power for 30 seconds. Stir, and heat again in 15-second bursts until the chocolate is smooth and melted.

2 Test the temperature and continue to heat in short bursts until it reaches 45°C (113°F). Let it cool until the temperature reaches 27°C (80°F), stirring frequently. The chocolate should remain at this temperature as you use it – warm it a little if it drops too low.

Over a hob

1 Melt chocolate pieces in a heatproof bowl over a pan of simmering water. The base should not touch the water.

2 Stir occasionally to distribute the heat. Heat until the sugar thermometer measures 45°C (113°F).

3 Remove from the heat and let it cool until the temperature reaches 27°C (80°F), stirring frequently.

CREATIVE CAKES, CUPCAKES, AND MUFFINS

Whizz up divinely soft sponges and pretty cupcakes for all your friends. Treat times will never be the same again with these irresistible loaves, moist muffins, and fruity cheesecakes!

Blueberry muffins

These light and fluffy muffins are topped with zingy lemon juice for an extra burst of flavour. They are best served warm.

Level rating 🧁

How long?   25 mins prep,
20 mins baking

How many?   12

Ingredients

60g (2oz) unsalted butter
280g (9½oz) plain flour
1 tbsp baking powder
pinch of salt
200g (7oz) caster sugar
1 egg
finely grated zest and juice of 1 lemon
1 tsp vanilla extract
250ml (9fl oz) milk
225g (8oz) blueberries

Special equipment

12-hole muffin tin
12 paper muffin cases

1 Preheat the oven to 220°C (425°F/Gas 7). Melt the butter in a pan over a medium-low heat.

2 Sift the flour, baking powder, and salt into a bowl. Set two tablespoons of sugar aside and stir the rest into the flour. Make a well in the centre.

3 In a separate bowl, beat the egg lightly until just broken down and mixed together. Add the melted butter, lemon zest, vanilla, and milk. Beat until foamy.

4 Pour the egg mixture into the flour. Then gradually stir it into the dry ingredients to make a smooth batter.

5 Gently fold in all the blueberries. Do not overmix, or the muffins will be tough.

6 Place the muffin cases in the tin. Spoon in the batter, fill each case to three-quarters full.

8 In a small bowl, stir the reserved sugar with the lemon juice until the sugar dissolves.

7 Bake for 15–20 minutes. Let the muffins cool slightly, then transfer them to a wire rack.

9 While the muffins are still warm, dip the crown of each into the sugar and lemon mixture.

Top tip

The muffins will keep in an airtight container for two days.

10 Set the muffins upright back on the wire rack and brush with any remaining glaze.

Pizza muffins

Cheese and pepperoni give these savoury muffins a delicious flavour. Instead of having something sweet, try nibbling on these when you're hungry.

Level rating

How long?   15 mins prep,
                25 mins baking

How many?   8–10

Ingredients

oil, for greasing
250g (9oz) plain flour
1 tsp baking powder
1 tsp dried oregano
115g (4oz) butter, melted
250ml (9fl oz) milk
2 eggs
2 tbsp tomato pizza sauce, plus
  extra for dipping
115g (4oz) mixed Cheddar
  and mozzarella cheese, grated
150g (5½oz) mini pepperoni, sliced

Special equipment

2 x 6-hole or 1 x 12-hole muffin tin

TRY THIS

To make a veggie version, replace the same quantity of mini pepperoni with pitted black olives, cut lengthways.

1 Preheat the oven to 190°C (375°F/Gas 5) and grease a muffin tin with oil.

2 Mix the flour, baking powder, and oregano in a bowl. Mix the butter, milk, eggs, and pizza sauce in a jug.

3 Pour the egg mixture into the flour mixture and lightly stir together. Then fold in the cheese and pepperoni.

4 Spoon the mixture into the muffin tin. Bake for 20-25 minutes, until golden.

Carrot crunch muffins

These sweet muffins topped with crunchy oats are super tasty! They are perfect to take along to a picnic or a party.

Level rating

How long? 20 mins prep,
25 mins baking

How many? 12

Ingredients

140g (5oz) plain flour
2 tsp baking powder
½ tsp bicarbonate of soda
85g (3oz) light brown sugar
50g (1¾oz) hazelnuts, chopped
1 tbsp poppy seeds
100g (3½oz) carrot, grated
60g (2oz) sultanas
½ tsp ground cinnamon
100g (3½oz) porridge oats
grated zest and juice of 1 large orange
200ml (7fl oz) buttermilk
1 egg, beaten
75g (2½oz) unsalted butter, melted
pinch of salt

Special equipment

2 x 6-hole or 1 x 12-hole muffin tins
12 paper cases

Top tip

For extra zing use lemons instead of oranges. Or make a hole in the mixture with your finger (at Step 5) and pop in a chunk of white chocolate for a gooey centre in the middle of each muffin.

1
Preheat the oven to 200°C (400°F/Gas 6).

2
In a large bowl, mix together the flour, baking powder, bicarbonate of soda, and sugar. Then stir in the nuts, poppy seeds, carrot, sultanas, cinnamon, oats, and orange zest.

3
In another bowl, mix the buttermilk, egg, butter, salt, and orange juice. Mix together well, then pour the wet ingredients into the dry.

4
Mix the wet and dry ingredients together. Don't mix it too much or the muffins won't end up light and fluffy.

5
Line the muffin tins with the cases. Spoon the mixture into the cases – filling them up about two-thirds of the way. Bake for 20–25 minutes. Move to a wire rack to cool.

Drizzle muffins

These bright and tasty lemon muffins are a real treat. They are perfect for a party or when you have friends over.

1 Preheat the oven to 190°C (375°F/Gas 5). Line the muffin tin with the muffin cases.

2 Juice and grate one lemon and retain the juice. Add the zest to a bowl with the flour, bicarbonate of soda, salt, sugar, and poppy seeds.

3 Beat the milk, egg, oil, and lemon juice in a jug, then pour the wet ingredients into the dry and stir until just combined.

4 Spoon the mixture into the cases. Bake for 20–25 minutes until well risen. Leave to cool on a wire rack.

5 In a small bowl, mix together the icing sugar, lemon zest and juice. Once the muffins have cooled, drizzle the icing over them.

Ingredients

2 lemons

275g (9½oz) self-raising flour

½ tsp bicarbonate of soda

½ tsp salt

100g (3½oz) caster sugar

2 tbsp poppy seeds

150ml (5fl oz) milk

1 egg, beaten

90ml (3fl oz) sunflower oil

For the icing

75g (2½oz) icing sugar

2 tsp lemon zest

2 tsp lemon juice

To decorate

2 tsp lemon zest

16 jellied lemon slices

Special equipment

12-hole muffin tin

8 paper muffin cases

zester (optional)

Decorate with LEMON ZEST and JELLIED LEMON SLICES.

FRESH AND LEMONY!

Creamy cupcakes

Topped with a big swirl of buttercream icing, these delicious vanilla cupcakes are perfect for a party.

Ingredients

200g (7oz) plain flour, sifted

2 tsp baking powder

200g (7oz) caster sugar

½ tsp salt

100g (3½oz) unsalted butter, softened

3 eggs

150ml (5fl oz) milk

1 tsp vanilla extract

For the icing

200g (7oz) icing sugar

1 tsp vanilla extract

100g (3½oz) unsalted butter, softened

sugar sprinkles, to decorate

Special equipment

2 x 12-hole cupcake tins

24 paper cupcake cases

piping bag and star nozzle

1 Preheat the oven to 180°C (350°F/Gas 4).

2 Put the flour, baking powder, sugar, salt, and butter in a bowl. Rub together with your fingers until it looks like breadcrumbs.

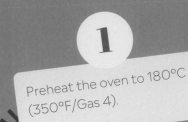

3 In another bowl, whisk the eggs, milk, and vanilla extract together until well blended. Slowly pour the egg mixture into the dry ingredients, whisking all the time.

4 Whisk slowly until smooth, being careful not to overmix. Pour all the cake batter into a jug to make it easier to handle.

5 Put the paper cases into the cupcake tins. Carefully pour the cake mixture into the cases, filling each one to half full. Bake for 20–25 minutes.

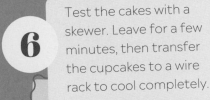

6 Test the cakes with a skewer. Leave for a few minutes, then transfer the cupcakes to a wire rack to cool completely.

7 For the icing, put the icing sugar, vanilla extract, and butter in a bowl. Beat with an electric whisk for five minutes until light and fluffy. Place in a piping bag fitted with a star nozzle.

8 Pipe by squeezing out the icing with one hand, while holding the cake with the other.

9 Starting from the edge, pipe a spiral of icing that comes to a peak in the centre.

10 Decorate the cakes with sprinkles. The cakes will keep in an airtight container for up to three days.

Pretty cupcakes

Top these simple cakes with pretty decorations and have fun with your colour combinations. Stacked in a tower, they are the perfect party treat.

Level rating

How long? 1 hr 15 mins prep,
2 days drying,
15 mins baking

How many? 12

Ingredients

100g (3½oz) unsalted butter, softened
100g (3½oz) caster sugar
100g (3½oz) self-raising flour
2 eggs, beaten
½ tsp vanilla extract

For the decoration and buttercream icing

cornflour, for dusting
200g (7oz) pink fondant
200g (7oz) white fondant
300g (10oz) unsalted butter, softened
600g (1lb 5oz) icing sugar, sifted
peach colouring paste or gel

Special equipment

fondant roller
butterfly plunger cutters, small and large
large flower plunger cutter
2 x 6-hole or 1 x 12-hole cupcake tins
12 paper cupcake cases
piping bag with large open star nozzle
12 lace cupcake wrappers

1 Dust a surface with cornflour. Roll out the pink fondant icing and white fondant icing. Use the plunger cutters to make butterfly and flower shapes.

2 Set aside to dry for two days. Place the butterflies in the middle of an open book. This will position the wings to be open as they dry.

34

3 Preheat the oven to 180°C (350°F/Gas 4). Line the cupcake tins with the cases. Put the butter, sugar, flour, eggs, and vanilla extract in a bowl and beat until creamy.

4 Divide the mixture between the paper cases. Bake for 15 minutes until golden and just firm. Cool in the tin for five minutes.

5 Move to a wire rack to cool completely.

6 For the buttercream icing, use an electric whisk to mix the butter with the icing sugar in a large bowl. Whisk until smooth and fluffy.

7 Using a palette knife, smooth half the icing onto six cupcakes. Top with fondant shapes.

8 For the six peach cupcakes, mix the food colouring paste into the remaining buttercream icing.

9 Put the peach icing in the piping bag, fitted with the large open star nozzle.

10 Pipe layers of icing in a spiral movement, making each layer slightly smaller as you go. Top with the fondant shapes. Place all the cupcakes in the lace wrappers before serving.

Cupcake owl

This creation is perfect for a party or family get-together. And you can make eight mini owls to sit alongside the big owl creation.

TWIT, TWOO

Level rating

How long?	1 hr 15 mins prep,
	15 mins baking,
	20 mins drying
How many?	24

Ingredients

150g (5½oz) unsalted butter, softened

150g (5½oz) caster sugar

½ tsp vanilla extract

3 eggs

150g (5½oz) self-raising flour

For the icing

200g (7oz) unsalted butter, softened

400g (14oz) icing sugar, sifted

yellow food colouring or gel

green food colouring or gel

To top the cupcakes

1 chocolate-covered sponge cake cookie,
   cut in quarters

200g (7oz) white chocolate buttons,
   reserve one to melt

75g (2½oz) chocolate-dipped pretzels,
   snapped into thirds

25g (scant 1oz) milk chocolate, grated

4 chocolate-covered sponge cake cookies,
   cut in half

2 large milk chocolate buttons

1 large milk chocolate button, cut in half

100g (3½oz) milk chocolate chips

Special equipment

2 x 12-hole cupcake tins

24 paper cupcake cases

1 Preheat the oven to 180°C (350°F/Gas 4). Put the paper cases in the cupcake tins.

2 Cream together the butter and caster sugar in a bowl using an electric whisk, until light and fluffy. Then beat in the vanilla extract.

3 Add the eggs, one at a time, beating well after each addition. Add a little flour after each addition if the mixture starts to curdle.

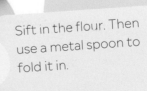

4 Sift in the flour. Then use a metal spoon to fold it in.

5 Spoon the mixture into the cases and bake for 15 minutes.

6 Cool the cupcakes on a wire rack.

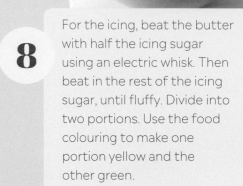

7 Use a sharp knife to carefully level off the top of each cupcake.

8 For the icing, beat the butter with half the icing sugar using an electric whisk. Then beat in the rest of the icing sugar, until fluffy. Divide into two portions. Use the food colouring to make one portion yellow and the other green.

9 Using a palette knife, cover the surface of 12 cupcakes with the yellow icing. Cover the remaining 12 cupcakes with the green icing.

10 To make the beak of the owl, take one quarter of the cookie and place it, chocolate-side down, on top of one of the green cupcakes. Place three white chocolate buttons beneath the cookie so that the buttons overlap each other.

11 For the claws, cut out V-shapes from two cookie quarters. Put a claw on two of the yellow cupcakes. Put pretzels beneath them. Cover two other yellow cupcakes with pretzels.

13 For the wings, take four green cupcakes and press two halves of the cookies on one side of each cupcake. Sprinkle grated chocolate on the remaining portion of each cupcake.

12 To make the body, cover three green cupcakes with white buttons. Take two more green cupcakes, cover half of their surface with the white buttons. Sprinkle grated chocolate on the remaining half of each.

14 For the eyes, place a large button in the middle of two yellow cupcakes. Dot melted white chocolate on each eye. For the ears, put half a large button on each cupcake. Put chocolate chips around the edges.

15 Put all the cupcakes on a table or large tray to make the owl, as shown on page 36.

TRY THIS

• Make eight baby owl cupcakes using the leftover cupcakes. Cut eight cookies in half and use them for the wings. Use another two cookies to make the beaks, by cutting small triangles from the cookies.

• Use 16 white chocolate buttons for the eyes. For the pupils, stick chocolate chips to the eyes, using leftover icing.

• Cut milk chocolate buttons in half for the ears, and grate milk chocolate onto the torso. If needed, use extra icing to hold the wings, beak, and ears in position.

Fudge cake balls

These bite-size treats are deliciously chocolatey and simple to make.

Level rating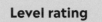

How long? 35 mins prep,
25 mins baking,
30 mins freezing

How many? 20–25

Ingredients

100g (3½oz) unsalted butter, softened,
  or soft margarine, plus extra for greasing
100g (3½oz) caster sugar
2 eggs
80g (2¾oz) self-raising flour
20g (¾oz) cocoa powder
1 tsp baking powder
1 tbsp milk, plus extra if needed
150g (5½oz) ready-made chocolate
  fudge icing
250g (9oz) dark chocolate
  cake covering
50g (1¾oz) white chocolate, broken
  into pieces

Special equipment

18cm (7in) round cake tin
food processor with blade attachment

1 Preheat the oven to 180°C (350°F/Gas 4). Grease the tin and line the base and sides with baking parchment.

2 Using an electric whisk, cream the butter and sugar until fluffy. Beat in the eggs one at a time, mixing well between additions, until smooth and creamy.

3 Sift together the flour, cocoa, and baking powder, and fold into the cake batter.

4 Mix in enough milk to thin the batter so that it will drop off a spoon.

5 Spoon into the tin and bake for 25 minutes until the surface is springy to the touch. Cool in the tin on a wire rack.

6 Whizz the cake in the processor until it looks like breadcrumbs. Put 300g (10oz) in a bowl. Add the fudge icing and blend together to a smooth, uniform mix.

7 Using dry hands, roll the cake mix into 20-25 balls, each the size of a walnut. Put the balls on a plate and freeze for 30 minutes until firm.

8 Line two baking trays with baking parchment. Melt the cake covering according to the directions on the packet. Put a few balls into the chocolate.

9 Using two forks, turn each ball in the chocolate until covered. Remove, allowing excess to drip off. Cover all the balls.

10 Put the coated cake balls on the baking trays to dry.

11 Melt the white chocolate in a heatproof bowl over a pan of simmering water.

12 Drizzle the white chocolate over the balls. Leave to dry completely before moving the balls to a serving plate.

KEEP in an AIRTIGHT CONTAINER for up to THREE DAYS.

Simple Victoria sandwich

Popular in Britain, this tasty cake is made up of jam and buttercream icing sandwiched between two layers of super-light and fluffy sponge.

Level rating

How long?   30 mins prep,
                  25 mins baking

How many?   6–8

Ingredients

175g (6oz) unsalted butter, softened, plus extra for greasing

175g (6oz) caster sugar

3 eggs

1 tsp vanilla extract

175g (6oz) self-raising flour

1 tsp baking powder

For the filling

50g (1¾oz) unsalted butter, softened

100g (3½oz) icing sugar, plus extra to serve

1 tsp vanilla extract

115g (4oz) good-quality seedless raspberry jam

Special equipment

2 x 18cm (7in) round cake tins

1

Preheat the oven to 180°C (350°F/Gas 4). Grease the tins and line with baking parchment.

2

Whisk the butter and sugar in a bowl for two minutes with an electric whisk, or until pale, light, and fluffy.

3

Add the eggs one at a time, mixing well between additions.

4

Add the vanilla and whisk briefly until well blended. Whisk the mixture for another two minutes until bubbles appear on top.

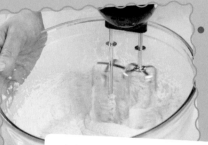

5

Sift the flour and baking powder into the bowl. With a metal spoon, gently fold in the flour until just smooth. Try to keep the mixture light.

6

Split the mixture evenly between the tins and smooth the tops with a palette knife. Bake for 20–25 minutes or until golden brown.

8 For the filling, beat together the butter, icing sugar, and vanilla until smooth.

7 Leave in the tins for a few minutes. Turn out, remove the parchment, and cool top side up on a wire rack.

9 Spread the buttercream icing evenly onto the flat side of a cooled sponge with a palette knife.

Top tip

The filled cake will keep in an airtight container in a cool place for up to two days.

10 Gently spread the jam on top of the buttercream using a table knife.

11 Top with the second sponge, flat sides together. Sift icing sugar on top to serve.

Chocolate cake

Everyone loves a rich chocolate cake, and in this recipe the yogurt in the mix makes it extra moist.

Level rating

How long? 30 mins prep, 25 mins baking

How many? 6-8

Ingredients

175g (6oz) unsalted butter, softened, plus extra for greasing

175g (6oz) soft light brown sugar

3 large eggs

125g (4½oz) self-raising flour

50g (1¾oz) cocoa powder

1 tsp baking powder

2 tbsp Greek yogurt or thick plain yogurt

For the chocolate buttercream

50g (1¾oz) unsalted butter, softened

75g (2½oz) icing sugar, sifted, plus extra to serve

25g (scant 1oz) cocoa powder

a little milk, if needed

Special equipment

2 x 18cm (7in) round cake tins

1 Preheat the oven to 180°C (350°F/Gas 4). Grease the tins and line with baking parchment.

2 Place the butter and sugar in a large bowl. Cream together with an electric whisk, until light and fluffy.

3 Crack in the eggs one at a time, beating after each addition, until well combined.

4 In a separate large bowl, sift together the flour, cocoa powder, and baking powder.

5 Fold the flour mixture into the cake batter until well blended, trying to keep it light.

6 Gently fold in the yogurt. This will help to make the cake moist.

Choose a fancy **PLATE** or **CAKE STAND** to serve the cake on.

7 Split the mixture between the two tins and smooth the tops. Bake for 20-25 minutes. Leave the sponges in their tins for a few minutes. Remove the parchment and put on a wire rack top side up.

8 For the buttercream, put the butter, icing sugar, and cocoa powder in a large bowl.

9 Blend the buttercream together with an electric whisk for five minutes or until fluffy.

10 If the cream is stiff, add milk, one teaspoon at a time, until it has a spreading consistency.

11 Spread the base of one sponge with the buttercream, then top with the other sponge. Sift the icing sugar over to serve.

Swiss roll

This tasty jam-filled cake is great to share with others. It's surprisingly easy to roll up and the swirl of jam inside looks very attractive.

Level rating

How long? 20 mins prep,
               15 mins baking

How many? 8–10

Ingredients

3 large eggs
100g (3½oz) caster sugar, plus extra
  for sprinkling
pinch of salt
75g (2½oz) self-raising flour
1 tsp vanilla extract

For the filling
6 tbsp raspberry jam (or any type you like)

Special equipment
32.5 x 23cm (13 x 9in) Swiss roll tin

1 Preheat the oven to 200°C (400°F/Gas 6). Line the base of the tin with baking parchment.

2 Put a heatproof bowl over a pan of simmering water. Add the eggs, sugar, and salt. Whisk with an electric whisk for five minutes until thick.

3 Test the egg mixture by checking if drips from the beaters sit on the surface for a few seconds. If they do, it's ready.

4 Carefully move the bowl from the pan to a work surface. Whisk for 1–2 minutes, until cool. Sift in the flour, add the vanilla extract, and gently fold in.

5 Pour the mix into the tin and gently smooth it into all the corners using a palette knife. Bake for 12–15 minutes until firm and springy to the touch.

6 The cake is ready when it has shrunk away slightly from the sides of the tin. Sprinkle a sheet of baking parchment larger than the tin evenly with a thin layer of caster sugar.

7 Carefully turn the cake out onto the caster sugar, so it lies upside down. Let it cool for five minutes, then peel the baking parchment from the cake.

8 For the filling, if the jam is too thick to spread, warm it gently in a small pan. Spread the jam all over the top of the cake with a palette knife.

9 Lightly press the back of a knife along one short side, 2cm (¾in) from the edge.

10 Using the pressed edge to start it off, gently but firmly roll the cake up, using the parchment.

11 Use the parchment to keep the cake tightly rolled and in shape. Let it cool, then unwrap the cake and place it on a serving plate, join downwards.

Sprinkle with CASTER SUGAR.

Top tip
The Swiss roll will keep in an airtight container for up to two days.

Chocolate chestnut roulade

The name roulade comes from the French word *rouler*, meaning to roll. A flat cake is covered with a sweet filling, before being rolled into a spiral.

Ingredients

butter, for greasing
35g (1¼oz) cocoa powder
1 tbsp plain flour
pinch of salt
5 eggs, separated into yolks and whites
150g (5½oz) caster sugar

For the filling

125g (4½oz) chestnut purée
30g (1oz) good-quality dark chocolate, broken into pieces
175ml (6fl oz) double cream
caster sugar, to taste (optional)

For decoration

125ml (4fl oz) double cream
50g (1¾oz) caster sugar
dark chocolate, grated with a vegetable peeler, to produce shavings

Special equipment

30 x 37cm (12 x 15in) Swiss roll tin
piping bag and star nozzle

1 Preheat the oven to 220°C (425°F/Gas 7). Grease the tin and line with baking parchment. Sift the cocoa powder, flour, and salt into a large bowl.

2 In another bowl, beat the egg yolks and 100g (3½oz) of the sugar using an electric whisk, until the mixture leaves a trail when you lift the beaters.

3 Clean the beaters. In a separate bowl, whisk the egg whites until stiff. Sprinkle in the remaining sugar and whisk again until glossy.

4 Sift about one-third of the cocoa mixture over the yolk mixture. Add about one-third of the egg whites.

5 Fold together lightly. Repeat with two more batches, until all the cocoa mixture and egg whites have been added.

6 Pour the batter into the tin and spread to the edges. Bake in the oven for 5–7 minutes.

7 Turn out onto a damp tea towel and peel off the parchment. Tightly roll up the cake within the damp tea towel. Leave to cool.

8 Put the chestnut purée in a bowl. Melt the chocolate in a heatproof bowl over a pan of simmering water. Stir the melted chocolate into the chestnut mixture.

9 Whip the cream in a separate bowl, until it forms soft peaks. Fold the chestnut mixture into the whipped cream. Add sugar to taste.

10 Unroll the cake onto a piece of parchment. Spread on the chestnut mix using a palette knife.

11 Using the parchment underneath, carefully roll up the filled cake as tightly as possible. Trim the edges with a serrated knife.

Decorate with the WHIPPED CREAM and CHOCOLATE SHAVINGS.

12 For the decoration, whip the cream and sugar until stiff. Fill the piping bag with the cream and decorate.

Zingy lemon polenta cake

This tasty wheat-free cake is packed with flavour and works just as well when made with wheat flour.

Level rating

How long?   30 mins prep,
                1 hr baking

How many?   8–10

Ingredients

175g (6oz) unsalted butter, softened, plus extra for greasing
200g (7oz) caster sugar
3 large eggs, beaten
75g (2½oz) polenta or coarse-ground cornmeal
175g (6oz) ground almonds
finely grated zest and juice of 2 lemons
1 tsp gluten-free baking powder
pared lemon zest, to decorate
thick cream or crème fraîche, to serve (optional)

Special equipment

22cm (9in) round springform cake tin
zester (optional)

1 Preheat the oven to 160°C (325°F/Gas 3). Grease the tin and line the base with baking parchment.

2 Cream the butter and 175g (6oz) of the sugar until fluffy. Gradually pour in the eggs, a little at a time, whisking well after each addition.

3 Add the polenta and almonds, and gently fold into the mix using a metal spoon.

4 Fold in the lemon zest and baking powder. The mixture will seem quite stiff.

5 Put the mixture into the tin and smooth the surface with a palette knife.

6 Bake the cake for 50–60 minutes until springy to the touch. Leave in the tin to cool for 10 minutes.

50

7 In a small saucepan, heat the lemon juice and remaining sugar over a medium heat, until the sugar has completely dissolved. Take off the heat.

8 Turn the cake out onto a wire rack, top side up. Leave on the parchment for now.

9 Using a thin skewer or cocktail stick, poke holes in the top of the cake while still warm.

10 Pour half of the hot lemon syrup over the surface of the cake a little at a time.

11 Once the syrup has soaked into the cake, pour the rest on. Serve the cake at room temperature, on its own or with thick cream or crème fraîche.

Decorate with strips of LEMON ZEST.

Carrot cake

This sweet and crunchy cake is topped with deliciously tangy orange icing.

Level rating

How long?   20 mins prep,
45 mins baking

How many?   8–10

1 Preheat the oven to 180°C (350°F/Gas 4). Grease the tin and line with baking parchment. Bake the walnuts on a baking tray for five minutes. Rub the nuts with a clean tea towel to take off any excess skin.

2 Pour the oil and eggs into a large bowl, tip in the sugar, and add the vanilla.

3 Using an electric whisk, beat the oil mixture until it is lighter and has noticeably thickened. .

 4 Squeeze the grated carrot thoroughly in a clean tea towel to remove excess liquid.

5 Gently fold the carrot into the cake batter, ensuring it is evenly mixed throughout.

Ingredients

225ml (7½fl oz) sunflower oil, plus
   extra for greasing
100g (3½oz) walnuts
3 large eggs
225g (8oz) soft light brown sugar
1 tsp vanilla extract
200g (7oz) carrots, finely grated
100g (3½oz) sultanas
200g (7oz) self-raising flour
75g (2½oz) wholemeal self-raising flour
pinch of salt
1 tsp ground cinnamon
1 tsp ground ginger
¼ tsp finely grated nutmeg
finely grated zest of 1 orange

For the icing

50g (1¾oz) unsalted butter, softened
100g (3½oz) cream cheese, at
   room temperature
200g (7oz) icing sugar
½ tsp vanilla extract
1 orange

Special equipment

22cm (9in) round springform cake tin
zester

6 Roughly chop the cooled walnuts and add to the mixture, along with the sultanas, and gently fold them in.

7 Sift over the two types of flour, then tip in any bran remaining in the sieve. Add the salt, spices, and orange zest, and fold all the ingredients together to combine.

8 Pour the cake mix into the tin and smooth with a palette knife. Bake for 45 minutes. Remove from the tin and take the baking parchment off. Cool on a wire rack.

9 Combine the butter, cream cheese, icing sugar, and vanilla in a bowl. Grate most of the zest of the orange into the bowl, reserving some for decoration.

10 Mix all the ingredients with an electric whisk until smooth, pale, and fluffy.

11 Using a palette knife, spread the icing over the cake. Make swirls for texture.

Use the ZESTER tool to make CURLS.

SUPER
MOIST

Zesty citrus cake

Bake and decorate this beauty in less than an hour.
The tangy orange taste adds a twist to a plain sponge.

Level rating

How long?

15 mins prep,
30 mins baking

How many?

8

Ingredients

175g (6oz) unsalted butter, softened,
  plus extra for greasing

175g (6oz) caster sugar

3 eggs, beaten

finely grated zest of 1 orange

1 tsp baking powder

175g (6oz) self-raising flour

For the icing

75g (2½oz) unsalted butter, softened

250g (9oz) icing sugar, sifted

zest of 1 orange, plus extra to decorate

2 tbsp orange juice

Special equipment

2 x 20cm (8in) cake tins

zester

1

Preheat the oven to 180°C (350°F/Gas 4). Grease the tins and line the bases with baking parchment.

Make sure to MIX IT WELL!

2

Put the butter, sugar, eggs, zest, baking powder, and flour in a large bowl, and beat together with an electric whisk until thick and well mixed.

3

Split the mix evenly between the tins and smooth the tops. Bake for 25-30 minutes.

4

Leave to cool in the tins for five minutes, then turn out onto a wire rack and let the cakes cool completely.

5

To make the icing, whisk the butter, icing sugar, zest, and juice in a bowl until smooth and creamy.

6

Spread half the icing on the flat side of one of the cakes. Lay the other cake on top, flat side down, and spread the remaining icing over it.

Use ORANGE PEEL to DECORATE.

Slice and enjoy!

Apple cake

This sweet cake is topped with *streusel*, the German word for a crumbly topping. It makes this simple cake even tastier!

Level rating

How long? 30 mins prep,
30 mins chilling,
50 mins baking

How many? 8

1 To make the topping, put the flour, sugar, and cinnamon in a mixing bowl.

Ingredients

175g (6oz) unsalted butter, softened, plus extra for greasing
175g (6oz) light muscovado sugar
finely grated zest of 1 lemon
3 eggs, lightly beaten
175g (6oz) self-raising flour
3 tbsp milk
2 dessert apples, peeled, cored, and cut into even, slim wedges

For the streusel topping

115g (4oz) plain flour
85g (3oz) light muscovado sugar
2 tsp ground cinnamon
85g (3oz) cold unsalted butter, diced

Special equipment

20cm (8in) loose-bottomed cake tin

2 Rub in the butter with your fingers to form a dough. Wrap in cling film and chill for 30 minutes.

3 Preheat the oven to 190°C (375°F/Gas 5). Grease the tin and line the base with baking parchment.

4 Whisk the butter and sugar in a mixing bowl until pale and creamy. Add the lemon zest and whisk slowly until well mixed.

5 Beat in the eggs, a little at a time, mixing well after each addition to avoid curdling.

6 Sift the flour into the batter and gently fold in with a metal spoon. Add the milk to the batter and gently mix it in.

7 Spread half the mixture in the tin and smooth with a palette knife. Put half the apple wedges over the mixture, overlapping them slightly.

8 Spread the rest of the mixture over the apples. Then put the remaining apples on the mixture, overlapping them slightly.

9 Coarsely grate the streusel dough and sprinkle it evenly over the top of the cake.

SERVE WARM

10 Bake for 45–50 minutes. Test it with a skewer to check it is cooked through.

11 Leave the cake to cool slightly in the tin for 10 minutes. Keeping the streusel on top, carefully remove the cake from the tin.

TO SERVE, transfer to a LARGE PLATE.

Rhubarb and ginger upside-down cake

Baked with the rhubarb at the bottom, this delicious dessert is turned upside down to serve.

Level rating 🧁🧁

How long? 40 mins prep, 45 mins baking

How many? 6–8

Ingredients

150g (5½oz) unsalted butter, softened, plus extra for greasing

500g (1lb 2oz) young, pink rhubarb

150g (5½oz) soft dark brown sugar

4 tbsp finely chopped, preserved stem ginger

3 large eggs

150g (5½oz) self-raising flour

2 tsp ground ginger

1 tsp baking powder

double cream, whipped, or crème fraîche, to serve (optional)

Special equipment

22cm (9in) round springform cake tin

1 Preheat the oven to 180°C (350°F/Gas 4). Grease the tin and line the base and sides with baking parchment.

2 Remove any dry ends of the stalks. Carefully cut the rhubarb into 2cm (¾in) lengths with a sharp knife.

3 Scatter a little of the sugar and a small amount of chopped ginger evenly over the base of the cake tin.

4 Lay the rhubarb in the tin, tightly packed, making sure the base is well covered.

5 Put the butter and remaining sugar into a large bowl. Cream the butter and sugar until light and fluffy.

6 Beat in the eggs one at a time, whisking as much air as possible into the mixture.

7 Gently fold the remaining chopped ginger into the mixture, until well mixed.

8 Sift together the flour, ground ginger, and baking powder into a separate bowl.

9 Gently fold the dry ingredients into the cake mixture.

Top tip

The cake is also good cold and will keep in a cool place in an airtight container for up to two days.

10 Spoon the cake mix over the rhubarb base. Bake for 45 minutes until springy to the touch.

11 Leave the cake to cool in the tin for 20–30 minutes, before carefully turning it out. Take the parchment off and serve warm, with double cream.

SUPER MOIST

Lemon drizzle loaf cake

This lovely loaf cake is both sweet and sour at the same time. It's easy to make, and best eaten once the lemon juice mixture has soaked into the cake.

Teatime treat!

Level rating

How long? 25 mins prep,
50 mins baking

How many? 8

Ingredients

200g (7oz) butter, softened, plus extra
   for greasing
finely grated zest and juice of 2 lemons
200g (7oz) caster sugar
3 eggs, beaten
200g (7oz) self-raising flour
1 tsp baking powder
2 tbsp milk
75g (2½oz) granulated sugar
85g (3oz) icing sugar

Special equipment

450g (1lb) loaf tin

1

Preheat the oven to 180°C (350°F/Gas 4). Grease the loaf tin and line the base with baking parchment.

2

Put the lemon zest, butter, and caster sugar in a mixing bowl and beat together with an electric whisk until the mixture is light and fluffy.

3

Whisk in the eggs a little at a time. Sift the flour and baking powder into the bowl. Add the milk and mix together well. Pour the mixture into the loaf tin.

4

Bake for 45-50 minutes or until a skewer comes out clean. Then, prick the top of the cake all over with a skewer. The holes will be filled in the next step.

5

Mix four teaspoons of the lemon juice with the granulated sugar. Drizzle the sugary juice over the cake so it sinks into all the holes. Allow the cake to cool before taking it out of the tin.

6

Combine the icing sugar with the rest of the lemon juice and mix until smooth. Drizzle the icing over the top, allowing it to run over the sides.

Banana bread

A mash of ripe bananas is delicious baked in this sweet quick loaf. Spices and nuts add an amazing flavour and crunch.

Level rating

How long?   25 mins prep, 40 mins baking

How many?   2 loaves

1 Preheat the oven to 180°C (350°F/Gas 4). Grease and flour both loaf tins thoroughly.

2 Sift the flour, baking powder, cinnamon, and salt into a large bowl. Mix in the walnuts. Make a well in the centre.

3 Beat the eggs in a separate bowl with a fork or hand whisk.

4 Mash the bananas with a fork in another bowl, until they form a smooth paste.

5 Stir the bananas into the egg mixture until well blended. Add the lemon zest and mix together.

6 Add the lemon juice, oil, both types of sugar, and vanilla. Stir until combined.

Ingredients

unsalted butter, for greasing

375g (13oz), strong white bread flour, plus extra for dusting

2 tsp baking powder

2 tsp ground cinnamon

1 tsp salt

125g (4½oz) walnut pieces, coarsely chopped

3 eggs

3 ripe bananas, chopped

finely grated zest and juice of 1 lemon

125ml (4fl oz) vegetable oil

200g (7oz) granulated sugar

100g (3½oz) soft brown sugar

2 tsp vanilla extract

cream cheese or butter, to serve (optional)

Special equipment

2 x 450g (1lb) loaf tin

7 Pour three-quarters of the banana mixture into the well in the flour, and stir well. Gradually blend in the remaining banana mixture. Stir until just smooth.

8 Spoon the mixture into the tins, dividing it equally. The tins should be about half full.

9 Bake for 35–40 minutes until the loaves start to shrink away from the sides of the tins. Test with a skewer. It should come out clean.

10 Let the loaves cool slightly in the tins, then transfer to a wire rack to cool completely.

Top tip

This bread will keep in an airtight container for up to three or four days.

Serve with BUTTER or CREAM CHEESE.

Baked berry cheesecake

This delicious cheesecake is so simple to make. Served with a sweet strawberry sauce, it is definitely fit for a party.

Level rating

How long?   45 mins prep,
1 hr 10 mins baking,
4 hrs chilling

How many?   8

Ingredients

75g (2½oz) unsalted butter, melted, plus extra for greasing

150g (5½oz) digestive biscuits, crushed into fine crumbs

For the filling

675g (1½lb) cream cheese, at room temperature

150ml (5fl oz) soured cream, at room temperature

150g (5½oz) caster sugar

1 tsp vanilla extract

pinch of fine sea salt

grated zest of ½ lemon

1 tbsp lemon juice

2 eggs

For the sauce

400g (14oz) strawberries, thinly sliced

1 tbsp lemon juice

1 tbsp caster sugar

4 tbsp strawberry jam, sieved to remove seeds

Special equipment

20cm (8in) deep springform cake tin

1 Preheat the oven to 180°C (350°F/Gas 4). Grease the base and sides of the tin and line with baking parchment. Combine the melted butter with the biscuit crumbs in a large bowl.

2 Tip the mixture into the tin. Using the back of a spoon, gently press it into the bottom of the tin to form an even layer. Bake for 10 minutes, then set aside to cool.

3 For the filling, whisk the cream cheese, soured cream, sugar, vanilla extract, salt, and lemon zest and juice in a bowl until combined. Add the eggs, one at a time, and whisk well to combine.

4 Cover the base and sides of the tin with foil and put it in a large roasting tin. Pour the filling over the biscuit base. Pour enough boiling water into the roasting tin to come halfway up the sides of the tin.

5 Bake for one hour. Turn off the oven and leave the cheesecake to cool in the oven for 30 minutes. Let it cool completely on a wire rack, then chill for at least four hours.

TRY THIS

Instead of using strawberries for the sauce, try using the same weight of raspberries, blueberries, or blackberries.

6 For the sauce, mix the strawberries, lemon juice, and sugar in a bowl, then leave for 30 minutes. Gently heat the jam in a small saucepan. Stir it into the strawberry mixture and leave to cool. Drizzle the sauce over the cheesecake to serve.

Top tip

The cheesecake will keep in the fridge, well wrapped in cling film, for up to three days.

Marbled chocolate cheesecake

This mouthwatering cheesecake is perfect for any special occasion. The marble effect is unique as it varies each time you make it.

Level rating

How long? 40 mins prep,
5 hrs chilling,
1 hr baking

How many? 8–10

Ingredients

75g (2½oz) unsalted butter, melted, plus extra for greasing

150g (5½oz) digestive biscuits, crushed

150g (5½oz) good-quality plain chocolate

500g (1lb 2oz) full-fat cream cheese, at room temperature

150g (5½oz) caster sugar

1 tsp vanilla extract

2 eggs

Special equipment

20cm (8in) deep springform cake tin

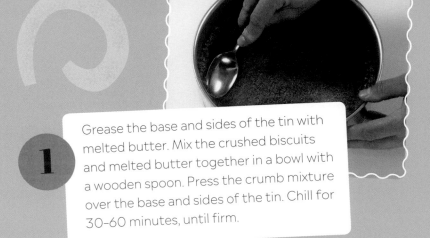

1 Grease the base and sides of the tin with melted butter. Mix the crushed biscuits and melted butter together in a bowl with a wooden spoon. Press the crumb mixture over the base and sides of the tin. Chill for 30–60 minutes, until firm.

2 Preheat the oven to 180°C (350°F/Gas 4).

3 Break the chocolate into chunks, then melt it in a heatproof bowl placed over a pan of simmering water, stirring occasionally, until smooth. Leave it to cool.

4 Beat the cream cheese in a bowl with an electric whisk for 2–3 minutes, until smooth. Add the sugar and vanilla extract, and beat again until smooth. Add the eggs one by one, beating well after each addition. Pour half of the filling into the biscuit base.

5 Once the melted chocolate has completely cooled, mix it into the remaining filling.

6 Carefully spoon the chocolate filling in a ring over the plain filling.

7 Using a table knife, swirl the fillings together to make a marbled pattern. Bake in the oven for 50–60 minutes, until the side is set. Turn the oven off and leave the cake in there until cool. Chill for four hours before serving.

TRY THIS

For an all-chocolate cheesecake, use 300g (10oz) plain or white chocolate, 100g (3½oz) sugar, and don't divide the mixture.

Top tip

This cheesecake can be made up to three days ahead, kept tightly wrapped in cling film in the fridge.

Blueberry ripple cheesecake

The marbled effect on this cheesecake is so easy to achieve and always looks magical. It is served with a *compote*, the French word for a fruity sauce.

Ingredients

50g (1¾oz) unsalted butter,
  plus extra for greasing
125g (4½oz) digestive biscuits
150g (5½oz) blueberries
150g (5½oz) caster sugar, plus 3 tbsp extra
400g (14oz) cream cheese
250g (9oz) mascarpone
2 large eggs, plus 1 large egg yolk
½ tsp vanilla extract
2 tbsp plain flour, sifted

For the compote

100g (3½oz) blueberries
1 tbsp caster sugar
squeeze of lemon juice

Special equipment

20cm (8in) deep springform cake tin
food processor with blade attachment
nylon sieve

1 Preheat the oven to 180°C (350°F/Gas 4). Grease the base and sides of the cake tin.

2 Put the biscuits in a food bag and crush with a rolling pin to make into crumbs. Melt the butter in a saucepan over a low heat. It should not begin to turn brown.

3 Add the crumbs to the pan and stir until they are coated in butter. Remove from the heat. Press the crumbs down into the base of the tin, using the back of a spoon.

4 Put the blueberries and three tablespoons of sugar in the processor. Whizz until smooth. Push the mix through the nylon sieve into a small pan. Boil and then simmer for 3-5 minutes. Carefully take off the heat.

5 Place the remaining sugar, cream cheese, mascarpone, eggs, yolk, vanilla and flour in the processor. Whizz until smooth. Pour the mix onto the biscuit base and smooth the top.

6 Drizzle over the berry mixture and make swirls by drawing a metal skewer through the mix.

7 Boil a kettle of water. Wrap the sides of the cake tin with foil. Put it in a deep roasting tray. Pour hot water into the tray, to come halfway up the cake tin.

8 Bake for 40 minutes until set, but a bit wobbly. Turn off the oven, open the door, and leave the cake inside the oven for one hour. Put the cake on a wire rack and take off the sides of the tin.

9 Use two cake slicers to move the cheesecake to a serving plate, and leave to cool completely.

10 Put all the ingredients for the compote in a small pan and heat it gently, until the sugar dissolves. Carefully transfer to a jug to serve.

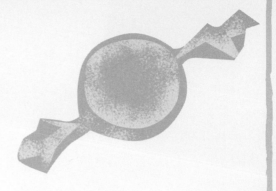

CELEBRATION CAKES

Create amazing "wow" bakes that will impress your friends and family. Perfect for parties and festive occasions, these luxurious layered cakes are rich, sweet, and full of surprises.

Triple-layer chocolate cake

If you are a chocolate lover, you will adore this cake. The rich sponge is topped with mouthwatering icing and delicious chocolate curls.

Ingredients

300g (10oz) unsalted butter, softened, plus
   extra for greasing
300g (10oz) golden caster sugar
300g (10oz) self-raising flour
4 tbsp cocoa powder
1 tsp bicarbonate of soda
5 large eggs
1 tsp vanilla extract
4 tbsp milk

For the icing and filling

175g (6oz) plain chocolate
450ml (15fl oz) double cream
30g (1oz) unsalted butter
1 tbsp caster sugar
a few drops of vanilla extract

Special equipment

3 x 20cm (8in) sandwich tins

1 Preheat the oven to 180°C (350°F/Gas 4). Lightly grease the tins and line the bases with baking parchment.

2 Put the butter and sugar in a large bowl and beat with an electric whisk until pale. Sift the flour, cocoa powder, and bicarbonate of soda into the bowl. Add the eggs, vanilla extract, and milk, then whisk for one minute, until the mixture is fluffy.

3 Divide the mixture evenly between the three tins and level the surface. Bake for 30–35 minutes, until the sponge springs back when lightly pressed. Leave the cakes to cool in the tins for five minutes, then move to a wire rack to cool completely.

4 To make the chocolate curls, break off 50g (1¾oz) of the chocolate. Carefully draw a vegetable peeler across the surface of the chocolate at an angle, so that curls of chocolate form. Set aside in a cool place.

5 Put the remaining chocolate and 150ml (5fl oz) of the cream in a heatproof bowl set over a pan of gently simmering water. Stir until the chocolate melts. Remove from the heat, stir in the butter, and leave to cool.

6 In a separate bowl, whisk the remaining cream, sugar, and vanilla extract with an electric whisk, until soft peaks form. Spread the cream on two of the cakes, stack them on top of each other, then top with the third cake.

7 Spoon the cooled chocolate icing over the top, allowing a little to drip down the sides of the cake. Scatter over the chocolate curls and serve.

Naked cake

A naked cake is easy to spot, with its bare layers and simple decoration. This one has tasty freeze-dried raspberries and lemon flavour that make it the ideal cake for any party.

Level rating

How long? 1 hr prep,
30 mins baking

How many? 12–14

Ingredients

350g (12oz) unsalted butter, cubed and
softened, plus extra for greasing

325g (11oz) caster sugar

finely grated zest of 2 lemons

6 eggs

350g (12oz) self-raising flour

2 tbsp milk

15g (½oz) freeze-dried raspberries, plus
extra to decorate

For the icing

150g (5½oz) unsalted butter, softened

finely grated zest of 1 lemon

300g (10oz) icing sugar

200g (7oz) mascarpone

2 tbsp lemon juice

fresh edible flowers, to decorate (optional)

Special equipment

3 x 20cm (8in) round cake tins

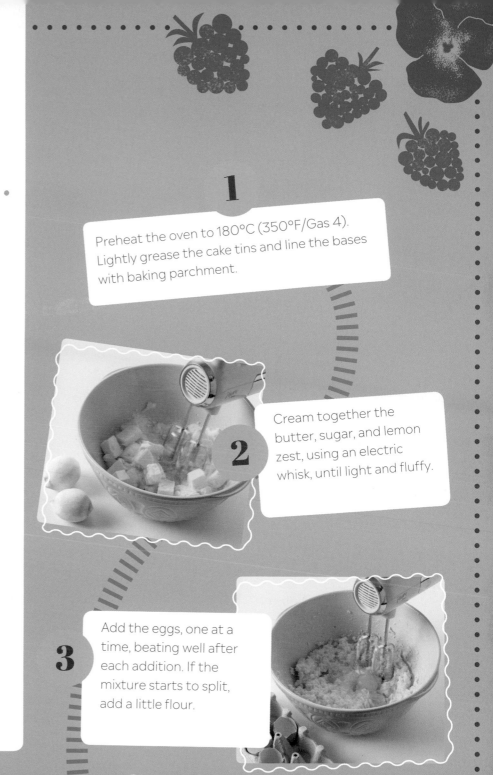

1
Preheat the oven to 180°C (350°F/Gas 4).
Lightly grease the cake tins and line the bases
with baking parchment.

2
Cream together the
butter, sugar, and lemon
zest, using an electric
whisk, until light and fluffy.

3
Add the eggs, one at a
time, beating well after
each addition. If the
mixture starts to split,
add a little flour.

4
Gently fold in the flour
using a metal spoon.

75

5 Stir the milk into the mixture, until well combined.

6 Scatter over the freeze-dried raspberries and mix them in evenly.

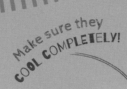

7 Divide the mixture equally between the tins, and level the tops using a spatula.

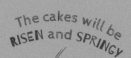
The cakes will be **RISEN** and **SPRINGY**.

8 Bake for 25–30 minutes, until the cakes are golden and springy to the touch. Swap the tins around in the oven after 15 minutes so they bake evenly.

Make sure they **COOL COMPLETELY!**

9 Put on wire racks to cool and take off the baking parchment.

10 For the icing, put the butter, zest, and half the icing sugar in a bowl, and beat together with an electric whisk until creamy.

11 Add the mascarpone, lemon juice, and remaining icing sugar, and beat until smooth and fluffy.

This gives the cake its **NAKED** look.

12 Once cooled, carefully level the cakes with a serrated knife. Place a slightly smaller cake tin base on top of each cake and use a sharp knife to cut round the edge of each cake.

13 Put a blob of icing onto a plate and sit one of the sponges on top. Spread with a third of the icing.

14 Top with the next sponge, spread on another third of the icing, then top with the last sponge. Spread the top thinly with the remaining icing.

15 Sprinkle over some extra freeze-dried raspberries and decorate with edible flowers, if using. Serve straight away.

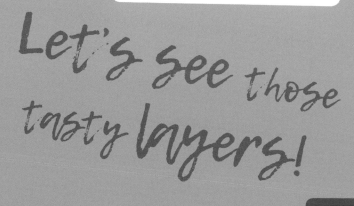

Let's see those tasty layers!

Piñata cake

Surprise your friends with this light and fluffy vanilla-flavoured sponge cake filled with delicious sweets. They won't be expecting goodies to be hidden inside!

Level rating

How long?	1½ hrs prep,
	30 mins baking,
	20 mins chilling
How many?	12–14

Ingredients

350g (12oz) unsalted butter, softened, plus
  extra for greasing
350g (12oz) caster sugar
2 tsp vanilla extract
6 eggs
350g (12oz) self-raising flour

For the icing, filling, and decoration

300g (10oz) unsalted butter, softened
600g (1lb 5oz) icing sugar, sifted
pink, orange, yellow, and blue food colouring
  gels or pastes
coloured sweets, to fill
cake bunting, to decorate (optional)

Special equipment

3 x 20cm (8in) round sandwich tins
3 x piping bags and star nozzles
7.5cm (3in) round cookie cutter

1 Preheat the oven to 180°C (350°F/Gas 4). Lightly grease the tins and line the bases with baking parchment.

2 Cream together the butter and caster sugar with an electric whisk, until light and fluffy. Then beat in the vanilla.

3 Add the eggs, one at a time, beating well after each addition.

4 Gently fold in the flour using a metal spoon.

5 Divide the mixture evenly in the three tins, weighing them to ensure they are equal. Bake for 25–30 minutes, until golden.

6 Take the cakes out of the tins, peel off the baking parchment, and cool on wire racks.

7 To make the icing, beat the butter with half the icing sugar, then beat in the rest, until light and fluffy. Add 1–2 teaspoons hot water to make it spreadable.

Be CAREFUL when CUTTING the CAKE.

8 When the cakes are cool, carefully level the tops using a serrated knife.

9 Cut out the centres of two of the cakes using the cookie cutter. You can make a small cake with the centres, or use them in a trifle.

SPREAD the ICING to the EDGES.

10 Mix a quarter of the icing with the pink colouring. Place the first ring onto a serving plate and sandwich together with the next ring, using a layer of pink icing. Put more pink icing on the second ring.

11 Fill the centre of the cake with the sweets. Place the remaining uncut cake on top to make the top level.

12 Spread the sides and top of the cake with a thin layer of plain icing, taking care not to get crumbs in the bowl of icing. Chill for 20 minutes. This helps the icing stick to the cake.

13 Spread a little more plain icing around the edge and over the top of the cake.

Choose DIFFERENT COLOURS if you LIKE.

14 Divide the remaining icing between three bowls and colour each bowl with a different food colouring. Put the icing into three piping bags that are each fitted with a star nozzle.

Use SWEETS to TOP the BUNTING POLES.

15 Pipe alternating colours of icing in a ring around the edge, on top of the cake. Stick the bunting on top to decorate, if using.

super sweet surprise!

Mini red velvets

These lovely little red cakes are made up of a light sponge and yummy cream cheese icing. Topped with fresh raspberries, they are perfect to show off at any special occasion.

Level rating

How long?   40 mins prep,
                  10 mins baking

How many?   8

Ingredients

100g (3½oz) buttery spread or unsalted
    butter, softened, plus extra for greasing
125g (4½oz) plain flour, plus extra for dusting
1 tbsp cocoa powder, sifted
½ tsp bicarbonate of soda
1 tsp baking powder
100g (3½oz) caster sugar
1 tsp vanilla extract
3–4 tsp red gel food colouring
1 large egg, beaten
100ml (3½fl oz) buttermilk
½ tsp distilled white vinegar

For the cream cheese icing

100g (3½oz) unsalted butter, softened
100g (3½oz) cream cheese
400g (14oz) icing sugar, sifted
1 tsp lemon juice
fresh raspberries or red sprinkles, to decorate

Special equipment

16 mini cake tins, about 6.5 x 2.5cm
    (2.5 x 1in), or 3 x 6-hole muffin tins
piping bag and star nozzle

1 Preheat the oven to 160°C (325°F/Gas 3). Lightly grease and flour the tins.

2 Put the flour, cocoa powder, bicarbonate of soda, and baking powder in a bowl and mix together.

3 In a separate bowl, cream together the butter and sugar with an electric whisk for 2–3 minutes, until light and fluffy.

4 Whisk in the vanilla and red food colouring until the colour is evenly blended. Whisk in the egg with a spoonful of the flour mixture.

5 Stir in half the buttermilk, then a spoon of the flour mixture. Alternate adding the buttermilk and flour mixture until all the ingredients are mixed in. Stir in the vinegar.

6 Spoon the mixture into the tins until half full (or less if using a muffin tin, only fill 16 holes). Bake for 8–10 minutes.

7 Let the cakes cool in the tins for a few minutes, then put on a wire rack. Leave them to cool completely before icing.

8 To make the icing, beat together the butter and cream cheese, then beat in the icing sugar a little at a time.

9 Once all the icing sugar has been added, whisk in the lemon juice until the mixture is paler in colour.

10 Use some of the icing to sandwich two of the cakes together. Repeat with the other cakes. Pipe the remaining icing on top of each cake. Decorate with raspberries or sprinkles.

Black Forest gâteaux

This traditional German cake is a mouthwatering blend of rich dark chocolate and sweet cherries. It definitely deserves its place on a celebration table.

Level rating

How long?   55 mins prep,
40 mins baking

How many?   8–10

Ingredients

85g (3oz) unsalted butter, melted, plus
   extra for greasing
6 eggs
175g (6oz) golden caster sugar
125g (4½oz) plain flour
50g (1¾oz) cocoa powder
1 tsp vanilla extract

For the filling and decoration

2 x 425g (15oz) cans pitted black cherries,
   drained, 10 tbsp juice reserved, and
   cherries from 1 can roughly chopped
600ml (1 pint) double cream
150g (5½oz) dark chocolate, grated

Special equipment

22cm (9in) round springform cake tin
piping bag and star nozzle

1 Preheat the oven to 180°C (350°F/Gas 4). Grease the tin and line the base and sides with baking parchment.

2 Put the eggs and sugar into a large heatproof bowl that will fit over a saucepan.

3 Place the bowl over a pan of simmering water. Don't let the bowl touch the water.

4 Mix with an electric whisk until the mixture is pale and thick, and will hold a trail from the beaters.

5 Remove from the heat and whisk for another five minutes or until cooled slightly.

6 Sift in the flour and cocoa. Gently fold into the egg mixture using a spatula. Fold in the vanilla and butter.

7 Pour the cake mixture into the tin and level the surface.

8 Bake for 40 minutes or until risen and just shrinking away from the sides.

9 Put on a wire rack, peel off the parchment, and cover with a clean cloth. Let it cool.

10 Carefully cut the cake into three layers. Use a serrated knife and long sweeping strokes.

11 Drizzle a third of the reserved cherry juice over each layer of the cake.

12 Whip the cream in a separate bowl until it just holds soft peaks; it should not be too stiff.

13 Place a layer of cake on a plate. Spread with the cream and half the chopped cherries.

14 Repeat with the second sponge. Top with the final sponge, right side up. Gently press down.

15 Cover the side with a layer of cream. Put the leftover cream in the piping bag.

16 Press grated chocolate onto the creamy sides using a palette knife.

17 Pipe a ring of cream swirls around the cake and place the whole cherries inside.

Top tip

The cake can be covered and kept in the fridge for up to three days.

Festive fruit cake

This recipe makes a wonderfully moist, rich fruit cake, ideal for Christmas, weddings, christenings, or birthdays.

Top tip

This cake will keep, un-iced, for up to eight weeks.

Level rating	
How long?	25 mins prep, overnight soaking, 2½ hrs baking
How many?	16

Ingredients

200g (7oz) sultanas
400g (14oz) raisins
350g (12oz) prunes, chopped
350g (12oz) glacé cherries
2 small dessert apples, peeled, cored, and diced
600ml (1 pint) apple juice
4 tsp dried mixed spice
200g (7oz) unsalted butter, softened
175g (6oz) soft dark brown sugar
3 eggs, beaten
150g (5½oz) ground almonds
280g (9½oz) plain flour, plus extra for dusting
2 tsp baking powder

For the icing

400g (14oz) ready-made marzipan
2–3 tbsp apricot jam
3 large egg whites
500g (1lb 2oz) icing sugar

Special equipment

20–25cm (8–10in) deep round cake tin

1 Put the sultanas, raisins, prunes, cherries, apples, juice, and spice in a saucepan.

2 Simmer over a medium-low heat and cover for 20 minutes until most of the liquid is absorbed.

3 Take off the heat. Leave overnight at room temperature for the fruits to fully absorb the liquid.

4 Preheat the oven to 160°C (325°F/Gas 3). Double-line the base and sides of the tin with baking parchment.

5 Using an electric whisk, cream the butter and sugar in a large bowl until fluffy.

6 Add the eggs, a little at a time, beating very well after each addition to avoid the mixture curdling.

7 Gently fold in the fruit mix and ground almonds, trying to keep volume in the mixture.

8 Sift the flour and baking powder into the bowl, and gently fold into the mixture.

9 Spoon the mixture into the tin, cover with foil, and bake for two and a half hours.

10 Test the cake is ready: a skewer inserted into the centre should come out clean.

11 Leave to cool, then turn out onto a wire rack to cool completely. Peel off the baking parchment.

12 Carefully trim the cake to level it. Transfer to a stand and hold in place with some marzipan.

13 Warm the jam and brush it thickly over the whole cake. This will help the marzipan stick.

14 On a lightly floured surface, knead the remaining marzipan until softened.

15 Roll out the softened marzipan until wide enough to cover the cake.

16 Drape the marzipan over the rolling pin and lift it over the cake.

17 With your hands or a smoother, gently ease the marzipan into place, smoothing out any bumps.

18 With a small sharp knife, carefully cut away any excess marzipan from the base of the cake.

19 Place the egg whites in a bowl and sift in the icing sugar, stirring well to combine.

20 With an electric whisk, beat the icing sugar mixture for 10 minutes until stiff.

21 Spread the icing over the cake with a palette knife and serve.

Painted cake

Get your paintbrush out, you're about to make an impressive edible work of art! This soft and fragrant cake is almost too beautiful to eat.

Perfect strokes

Top tip
Make sure to buy edible gold leaf and gold glitter.

Level rating

How long?   1 hr 15 mins prep,
25 mins baking,
35 mins chilling

How many?   12–14

Ingredients

300g (10oz) unsalted butter, softened and
   cubed, plus extra for greasing
300g (10oz) caster sugar
1 tsp rosewater extract
6 eggs
175g (6oz) self-raising flour
1 tsp baking powder
125g (4½oz) ground almonds

For the icing

300g (10oz) unsalted butter, softened
600g (1lb 5oz) icing sugar, sifted
1 tsp rosewater extract
pink, red, orange, and yellow food colouring
   or gel
edible gold leaf, to decorate
edible gold glitter, to decorate
dried rose petals, to decorate

Special equipment

3 x 18cm (7in) round cake tins
icing scraper
paintbrush, new and clean

1

Preheat the oven to 180°C (350°F/Gas 4). Lightly grease the tins and line the bases with baking parchment.

2

Cream together the butter and caster sugar, using an electric whisk, until light and fluffy. Then beat in the rosewater extract.

3

Add the eggs, one at a time, beating well using an electric whisk to combine. Add a little flour after each addition if the mixture starts to curdle.

4

Using a metal spoon, fold in the flour, baking powder, and ground almonds.

5 Divide the mixture equally between the three tins. Bake for 20–25 minutes until golden and springy.

6 Let the cakes cool in the tins for 10 minutes, then peel off the baking parchment and cool on wire racks.

7 To make the icing, beat the butter with half the icing sugar, using an electric whisk, then beat in the rest of the icing sugar, until light and fluffy. Mix in one teaspoon of rose water extract and 1–2 teaspoons of hot water to make it spreadable.

8 Take a quarter of the icing and add some pink food colouring until you have a soft pink icing.

ONLY take a THIN LAYER OFF the TOP.

9 When the cakes are cool, carefully level the tops, using a serrated knife.

SPREAD to the EDGES using a PALETTE KNIFE.

10 Ice the bottom sponge with a third of the pink icing. Place the next sponge on top and ice it with another third of the pink icing. Place the final sponge on top, but do not ice it.

11 Thinly cover the outside and top of the cake with some of the plain icing, then scrape off the excess with an icing scraper and discard. Chill in the fridge for 20 minutes to firm up.

12 Use the plain icing to cover the cake with a final coat, smoothing the sides and top again with an icing scraper. Chill for a further 15 minutes.

13 Divide the remaining plain icing between three small bowls. Use the food colouring to make one red, one orange, and one yellow.

14 Using a small palette knife, put splodges of icing on the sides and top of the cake. Try to alternate the four colours.

15 Smooth the sides with an icing scraper so the colours start to merge, then smooth the top.

Pretty palette

16 Use the paintbrush to add pieces of gold leaf. Spray the gold glitter and sprinkle the dried rose petals over the top of the cake.

Ice cream cone drip cake

Trick everyone with this clever party cake. The shiny icing flowing from the upside down cone makes it appear that ice cream is spilling everywhere. Have a napkin at the ready!

TASTY, GOOEY TREAT

Level rating 🧁🧁🧁🧁

How long? 1 hr 15 mins prep,
25 mins baking,
45 mins chilling

How many? 12–14

Ingredients

300g (10oz) unsalted butter, softened, plus
    extra for greasing
300g (10oz) caster sugar
2 tsp vanilla extract
6 eggs
300g (10oz) self-raising flour
1 tsp baking powder

For the buttercream icing

300g (10oz) softened unsalted butter
600g (1lb 5oz) icing sugar, sifted
1 tsp raspberry or strawberry flavouring
blue food colouring or gel

For the ganache drip icing

150g (5½oz) cook's white chocolate, broken
    into pieces
100ml (3½fl oz) double cream
1 tsp raspberry or strawberry flavouring
pink food colouring or gel

To top the cake

ice cream cone
1–2 tbsp sugar strands

Special equipment

3 x 20cm (8in) round cake tins

1
Preheat the oven to 180°C (350°F/Gas 4).
Lightly grease the tins and line the bases with
baking parchment.

2
Cream together the
butter and caster sugar,
using an electric whisk,
until light and fluffy.
Then beat in the
vanilla extract.

3
Add the eggs, one at a
time, beating well after
each addition. Add a little
flour after each addition
if the mixture starts
to curdle.

4
Sift in the flour and
baking powder. Then
use a metal spoon to
fold them in.

5 Divide the mixture equally between the three tins, weighing to ensure they are equal. Bake for 20-25 minutes until golden.

6 Let the cakes cool in the tins for 10 minutes, then remove the baking parchment and cool on a wire rack.

7 For the buttercream icing, beat the butter with half the icing sugar, using an electric whisk. Then beat in the rest of the icing sugar, until light and fluffy.

8 Add the flavouring and enough blue colouring to make a bright blue icing. Add 1-2 teaspoons of hot water to make it spreadable.

MAKE it as FLAT as you can.

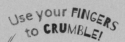

Use your FINGERS to CRUMBLE!

9 When the cakes are cool, carefully level the tops, using a serrated knife. Keep the cake pieces.

10 Crumble 60g (2oz) of the cake tops into a bowl, then add 2-3 tablespoons of the buttercream icing and stir gently to combine.

11 Using an ice cream scoop, shape the crumbled cake mixture into a ball, place on a small plate and chill for 10 minutes.

12 Divide a third of the icing between two of the cooled sponges. Spread to the edges with a palette knife. Stack the cakes in three tiers with the un-iced one on top.

13 Thinly cover the outside and top of the cake with a bit more icing, then scrape off the excess with a palette knife, and discard. Chill in the fridge for 20 minutes to firm up.

14 Move the cake to a serving plate before icing. Use most of the buttercream to cover the cake with a final coat, smoothing the sides and top using a palette knife.

15 Spread a layer of the buttercream icing over the cake ball and chill for 10 minutes.

16 For the ganache icing, place the chocolate and cream in a small saucepan and cook over a low heat, stirring until the chocolate has melted.

17 Take off the heat and stir in the flavouring and enough pink colour to make a bright pink shiny icing. Let it cool for 3–4 minutes, to thicken.

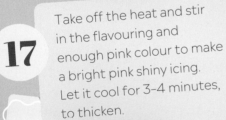

18 Put the cake ball on top, then spoon over a little of the ganache icing to cover. Spoon the remaining icing over the top of the cake, so it starts to drip down the sides.

19 Scatter the sugar strands over the cake ball and at the bottom of the cake. Put an ice cream cone at an angle on top of the ball. Let it set in a cool place (not the fridge) for 20 minutes before slicing.

PASTRIES, PIES, AND TARTS

Show off your cooking skills with creamy profiteroles and perfectly flaky pastries that melt in your mouth! Jazz up picnics and lunches with flavour-filled pies, hearty pasties, and impressive mini tartlets.

Chocolate profiteroles

The perfect choux pastry is always light and fluffy. Make these delicious buns, drizzled with chocolate sauce, as a dessert or party dish.

Level rating

How long?   30 mins prep,
22 mins baking

How many?   18

Ingredients

60g (2oz) plain flour

50g (1¾oz) unsalted butter

2 eggs, beaten

For the filling and topping

400ml (14fl oz) double cream

200g (7oz) good-quality dark chocolate, broken into pieces

25g (scant 1oz) unsalted butter

2 tbsp golden syrup

Special equipment

2 piping bags with a 1cm (½in) plain nozzle and 5mm (¼in) star nozzle

Serve the BUNS on a smart plate or cake stand.

1

Preheat the oven to 220°C (425°F/Gas 7). Line two large baking sheets with baking parchment.

2

Sift the flour into a large bowl, holding the sieve up high to get air into the flour.

3

Put the butter and 150ml (5fl oz) water into a small saucepan and heat gently until melted.

4

Bring to the boil, take off the heat, and tip in the flour all at once.

5

Beat with a wooden spoon until smooth. The mixture should form a ball. Cool for 10 minutes.

6 Gradually add the eggs, beating very well after each addition.

7 Continue adding the eggs, little by little, to form a stiff, smooth, and shiny paste.

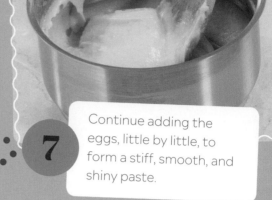

8 Spoon the mixture into a piping bag fitted with a 1cm (½in) plain nozzle.

9 Pipe 18 walnut-sized rounds onto the lined baking sheets, set well apart. Bake for 20 minutes until risen and golden.

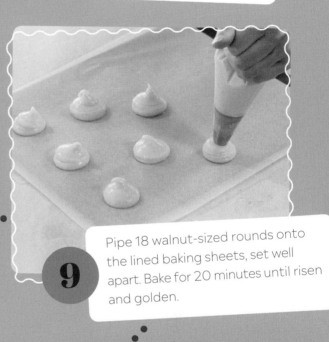

Top tip

The unfilled buns will keep in an airtight container for up to two days.

10 Take the pastry out of the oven and slit the side of each bun to allow the steam to escape.

11 Put the buns back in the oven for two minutes, to crisp, then put on a wire rack to cool completely.

12 Before serving, pour 100ml (3½fl oz) of the cream into a pan. Whip the rest of the cream until it forms soft peaks.

13 Add the chocolate, butter, and syrup to the cream in the pan, and heat gently until melted.

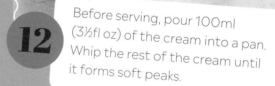

14 Put the whipped cream into a piping bag fitted with a 5mm (¼in) star nozzle.

15 Put the buns on a serving plate. Fill them with the whipped cream. Drizzle the chocolate mixture over them and serve immediately.

SWEET AND CREAMY

Croissants

Although these French pastries take some time to make, the final result is well worth the effort. Start making them the day before you wish to serve.

Level rating 🧁🧁🧁

How long? 1 hr prep, 5 hrs chilling, plus overnight chilling, 1 hr rising, 20 mins baking

How many? 12

serve with *jam*

Ingredients

300g (10oz) strong white bread flour, plus extra for dusting

½ tsp salt

30g (1oz) caster sugar

2½ tsp dried yeast

vegetable oil, for greasing

250g (9oz) unsalted butter, chilled

1 egg, beaten

jam, to serve

Top tip

The croissants will keep in an airtight container for up to two days. Gently reheat to serve.

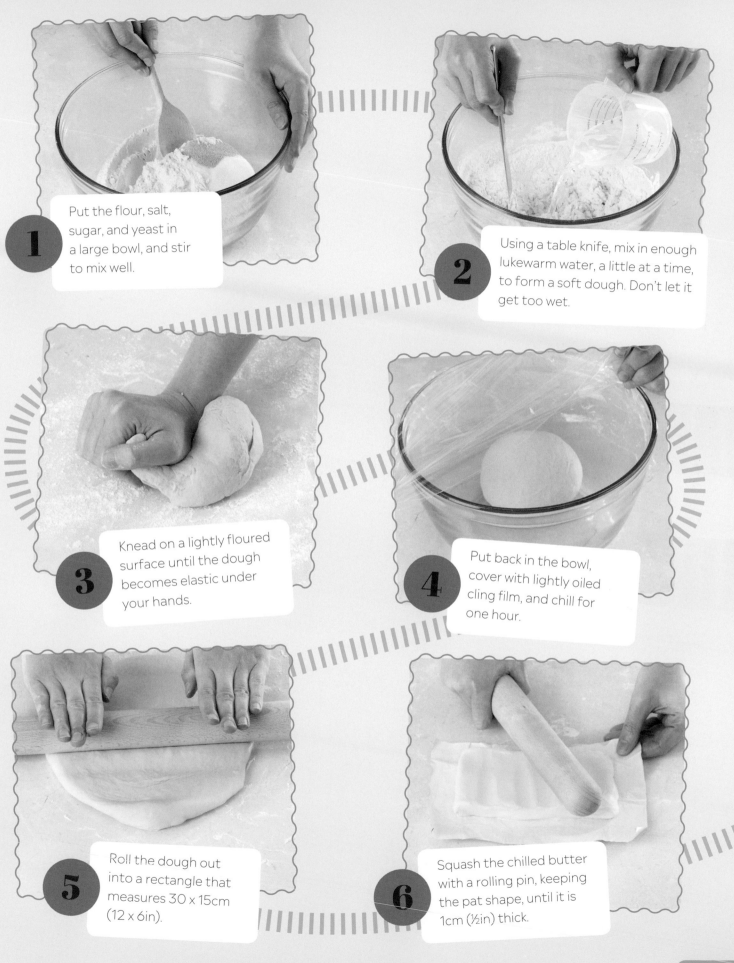

1 Put the flour, salt, sugar, and yeast in a large bowl, and stir to mix well.

2 Using a table knife, mix in enough lukewarm water, a little at a time, to form a soft dough. Don't let it get too wet.

3 Knead on a lightly floured surface until the dough becomes elastic under your hands.

4 Put back in the bowl, cover with lightly oiled cling film, and chill for one hour.

5 Roll the dough out into a rectangle that measures 30 x 15cm (12 x 6in).

6 Squash the chilled butter with a rolling pin, keeping the pat shape, until it is 1cm (½in) thick.

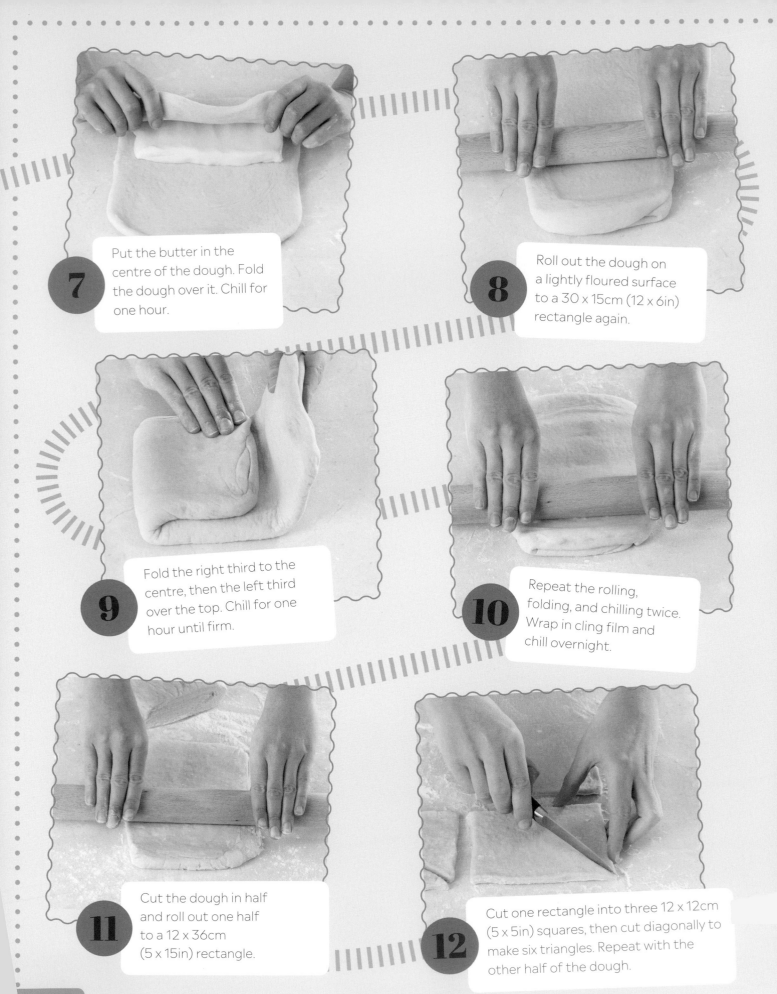

7 Put the butter in the centre of the dough. Fold the dough over it. Chill for one hour.

8 Roll out the dough on a lightly floured surface to a 30 x 15cm (12 x 6in) rectangle again.

9 Fold the right third to the centre, then the left third over the top. Chill for one hour until firm.

10 Repeat the rolling, folding, and chilling twice. Wrap in cling film and chill overnight.

11 Cut the dough in half and roll out one half to a 12 x 36cm (5 x 15in) rectangle.

12 Cut one rectangle into three 12 x 12cm (5 x 5in) squares, then cut diagonally to make six triangles. Repeat with the other half of the dough.

13 Holding the ends of the longest side of a triangle, roll it towards you. Curve into semi-circle shapes.

14 Line two baking trays with baking parchment and place the croissants on the trays, leaving space between each.

15 Cover with lightly oiled cling film. Leave for one hour until doubled in size. Remove the cling film.

16 Preheat the oven to 220°C (425°F/Gas 7). Brush the croissants with the egg, then bake for 10 minutes.

17 Lower the temperature to 190°C (375°F/Gas 5) and bake for another 5–10 minutes, until golden.

Rich and buttery!

Danish pastries

These tasty pastries are sweeter than the classic croissant. And the home-baked flavour is just too good to resist!

sweet treats

Ingredients

150ml (5fl oz) lukewarm milk

2 tsp dried yeast

30g (1oz) caster sugar

2 eggs, plus 1 egg for glazing

475g (1lb 1oz) strong white bread flour, sifted, plus extra for dusting

½ tsp salt

vegetable oil, for greasing

250g (9oz) chilled butter

200g (7oz) good-quality cherry, strawberry, or apricot jam

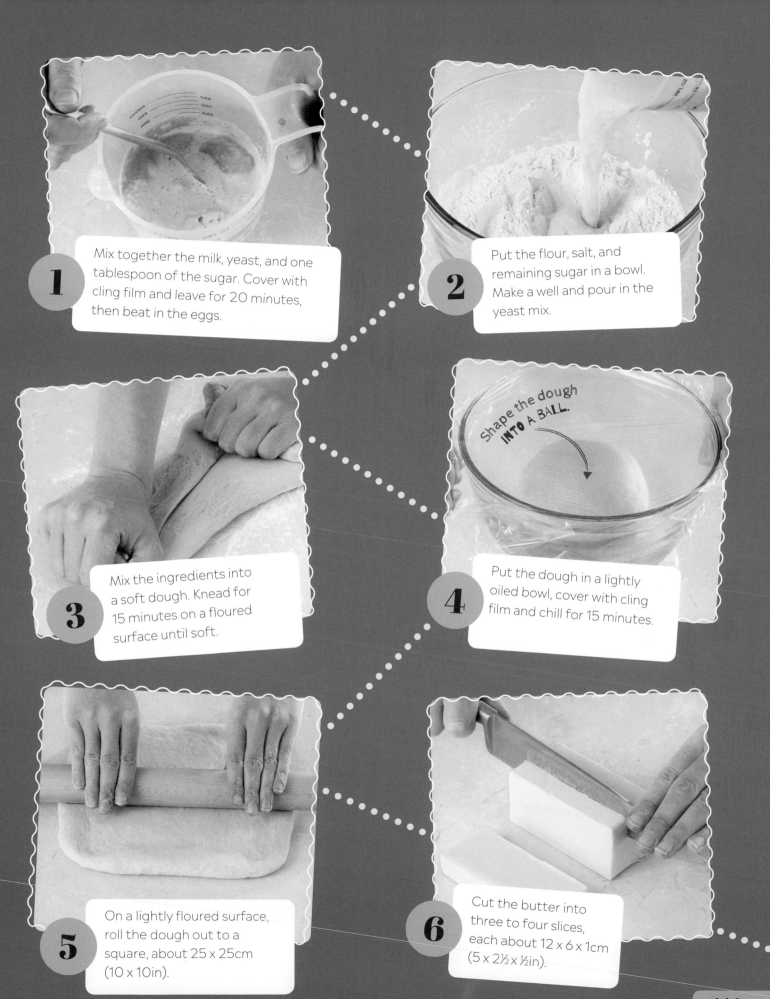

1 Mix together the milk, yeast, and one tablespoon of the sugar. Cover with cling film and leave for 20 minutes, then beat in the eggs.

2 Put the flour, salt, and remaining sugar in a bowl. Make a well and pour in the yeast mix.

3 Mix the ingredients into a soft dough. Knead for 15 minutes on a floured surface until soft.

Shape the dough
INTO A BALL.

4 Put the dough in a lightly oiled bowl, cover with cling film and chill for 15 minutes.

5 On a lightly floured surface, roll the dough out to a square, about 25 x 25cm (10 x 10in).

6 Cut the butter into three to four slices, each about 12 x 6 x 1cm (5 x 2½ x ½in).

7 Lay the butter slices on one half of the dough, leaving a border of 1–2cm (½–¾in).

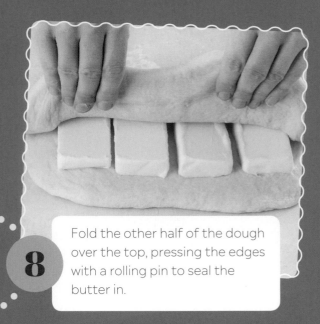

8 Fold the other half of the dough over the top, pressing the edges with a rolling pin to seal the butter in.

9 Generously flour and roll the dough into a rectangle three times as long as it is wide, and 1cm (½in) thick.

10 Fold the top third down into the middle, then the bottom third back over it.

11 Wrap in cling film and chill for 15 minutes. Repeat steps 9–10 twice, chilling for 15 minutes each time. Then cut the dough in half.

12 Roll each half on a floured surface to 30 x 30cm (12 x 12in) squares, 5mm–1cm (¼–½in) thick. Cut these into nine 10 x 10cm (4 x 4in) squares, making 18 squares in total.

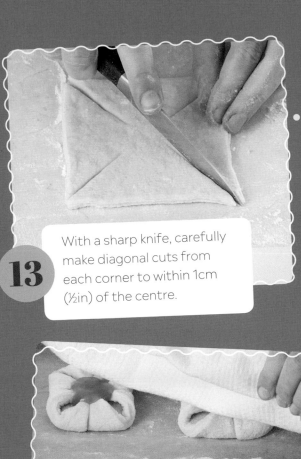

13 With a sharp knife, carefully make diagonal cuts from each corner to within 1cm (½in) of the centre.

14 Put one teaspoon of jam in the centre of each square and fold each corner into the centre.

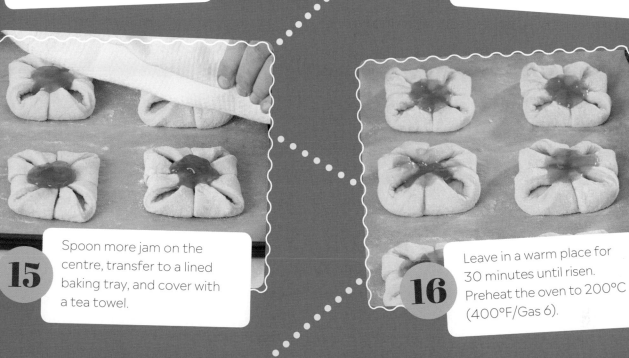

15 Spoon more jam on the centre, transfer to a lined baking tray, and cover with a tea towel.

16 Leave in a warm place for 30 minutes until risen. Preheat the oven to 200°C (400°F/Gas 6).

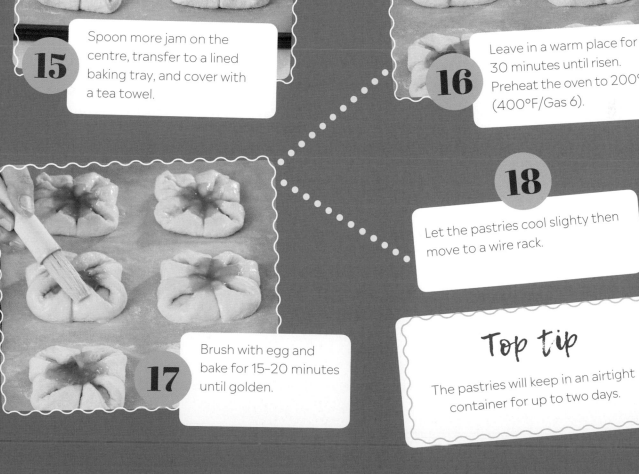

18 Let the pastries cool slightly then move to a wire rack.

17 Brush with egg and bake for 15–20 minutes until golden.

Top tip

The pastries will keep in an airtight container for up to two days.

Apple jalousie

In France, a *jalousie* is a type of window shutter. The top of this delicious pastry is sliced to look like a shutter, showing the apple inside.

Level rating

How long? 1½ hrs prep, 1 hr 15 mins chilling, 40 mins baking

How many? 6–8

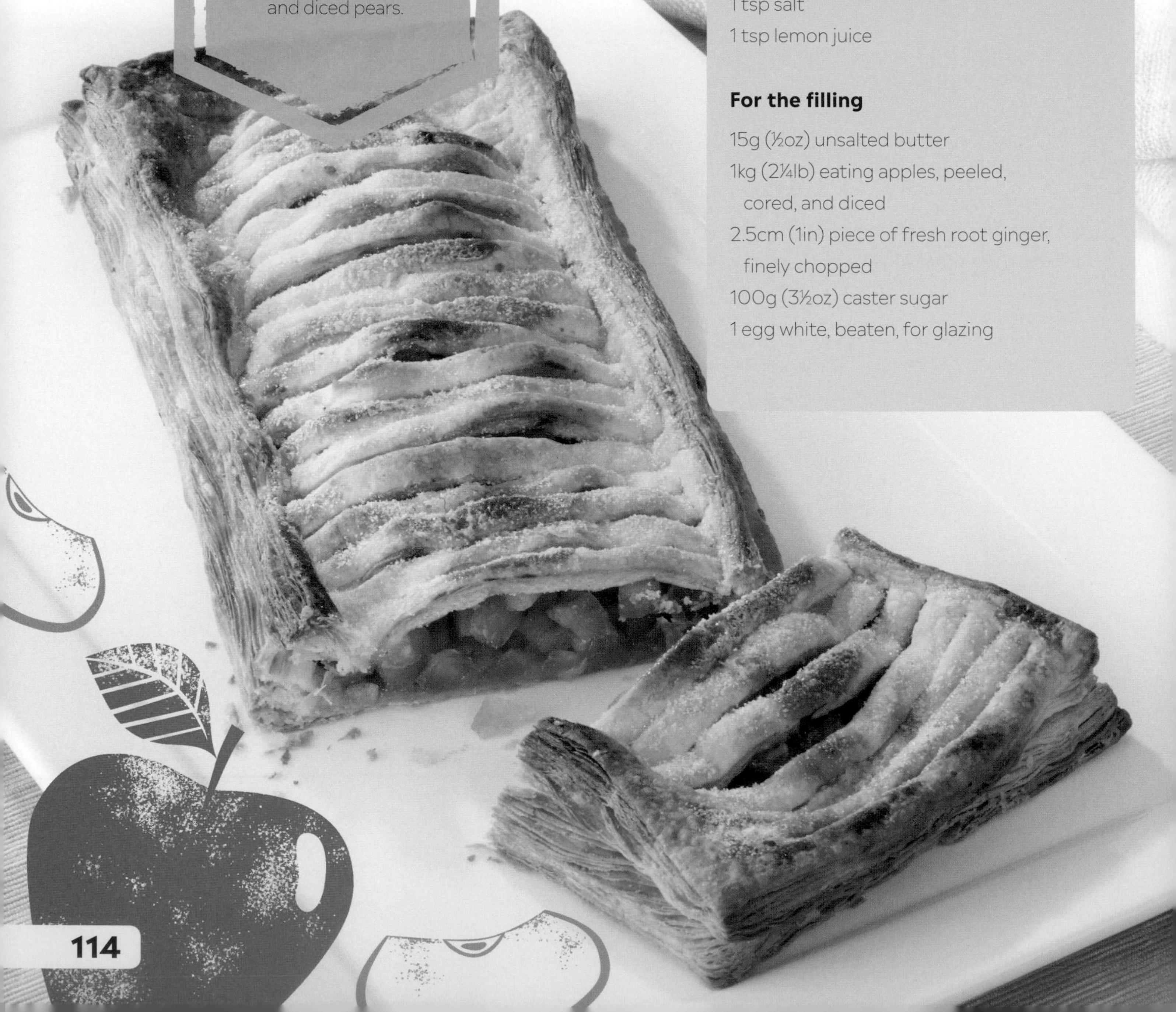

Ingredients

250g (9oz) unsalted butter, frozen for 30 minutes
250g (9oz) plain flour, sifted, plus extra for dusting
1 tsp salt
1 tsp lemon juice

For the filling

15g (½oz) unsalted butter
1kg (2¼lb) eating apples, peeled, cored, and diced
2.5cm (1in) piece of fresh root ginger, finely chopped
100g (3½oz) caster sugar
1 egg white, beaten, for glazing

TRY THIS

If you want to make this with a different fruit, then replace the same quantity of apples for peeled, cored, and diced pears.

1 Grate the butter into a bowl. Sift over the flour and salt. Rub together with your fingertips until crumbly.

2 Pour in 90–100ml (3–3½fl oz) cold water and the lemon juice. Use your hands to form a rough dough.

3 Put the dough on a floured surface. Work into a ball, then flatten it slightly.

4 Put the dough into a plastic bag and chill for 20 minutes.

5 On a floured surface, roll out the dough to a long rectangle, short sides 25cm (10in) in length.

6 Take one-third of the pastry and fold into the middle. Fold over the remaining third.

7 Turn it over so the joins are easily sealed when it is re-rolled.

8 Roll in the longer direction to a similar size as the original rectangle. Keep the short sides even in size.

9 Repeat the folding and rolling once more. Return it to the bag and chill for 20 minutes.

10 Roll and fold the pastry twice more, then chill for a final 20 minutes.

11 In a pan, melt the butter. Add the apples, ginger, and all but two tablespoons of the sugar.

12 Fry and stir for 15–20 minutes until the apples are soft and golden. Let it cool.

13 Roll out the pastry on a floured surface to 28 x 32cm (11 x 13in). Cut in half to make two 14 x 32cm (5½ x 13in) rectangles.

14 Fold one half lengthways and cut across the fold at 5mm (¼in) gaps, leaving a border on one side.

15 Put the uncut dough on a non-stick baking sheet and spoon the apple along the centre. Brush the edges with a little water.

16 Unfold the cut dough and place on top of the apples. Press the edges to seal together. Chill for 15 minutes. Preheat the oven to 220°C (425°F/Gas 7).

17 Bake for 20–25 minutes. Then brush with the egg white and sprinkle over the remaining sugar.

Top tip

To prepare ahead, the jalousie can be frozen at Step 16.

18 Put back in the oven and continue baking for 10–15 minutes. Serve the slices warm or at room temperature.

Cinnamon palmiers

These curly cinnamon-spiced pastries were given their name because of their shape. In French *palmier* means "palm tree". They are super tasty and make a breakfast extra special.

Top tip

The palmiers will keep in an airtight container for up to three days.

Level rating

How long?

45 mins prep,

1 hr 10 mins chilling,

30 mins baking

How many?

24

Ingredients

250g (9oz) unsalted butter, frozen
   for 30 minutes

250g (9oz) plain flour, plus extra
   for dusting

1 tsp salt

1 egg, lightly beaten, for glazing

For the filling

100g (3½oz) unsalted butter, softened

100g (3½oz) soft light brown sugar

4–5 tsp ground cinnamon, to taste

1 Grate the butter into a bowl. Sift over the flour and salt. Rub together with your fingertips, until crumbly.

2 Pour in 90–100ml (3–3½fl oz) cold water. Use a fork, then your hands to form a rough dough.

3 Put the dough into a plastic bag and chill for 20 minutes.

4 On a floured surface, thinly roll it out to a long rectangle, short sides 25cm (10in) in length.

5 Take one-third of the pastry and fold into the middle. Fold over the remaining third.

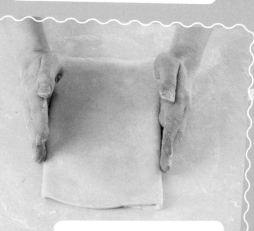

6 Turn it over so the joins are easily sealed when it is re-rolled.

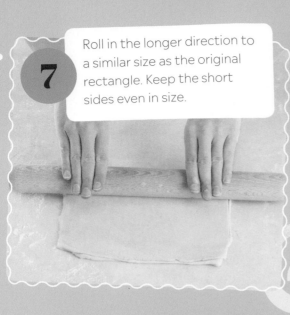

7 Roll in the longer direction to a similar size as the original rectangle. Keep the short sides even in size.

8 Repeat the folding and rolling once more. Put back in the bag and chill for 20 minutes.

9 Roll and fold the pastry twice more, then chill for a final 20 minutes.

10 Make the filling by beating together the butter, sugar, and cinnamon.

11 Preheat the oven to 200°C (400°F/Gas 6). Line two baking sheets with baking parchment.

12 Roll the dough out once again, so that the long edge measures 48cm (19in). Trim the edges. Spread the filling thinly over the surface.

13 Loosely roll one of the long sides into the middle, and repeat with the other side.

14 Brush with the egg, press together, then turn over and chill for 10 minutes.

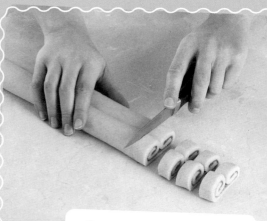

15 Carefully cut into 24 pieces, 2cm (¾in) thick. Then turn the palmiers face up.

16 Squeeze them to form an oval, and press down lightly with your palm to flatten slightly. Put on the lined baking sheets.

17 Brush the palmiers with the beaten egg and bake for 25–30 minutes.

18 They are ready when golden brown, puffed up, and crisp in the centre. Put on a wire rack to cool before serving.

Simple strudel

This sweet pastry is a traditional European dessert. *Strudel* is German for "whirlpool", because when it is cut open you can see swirls of pastry filled with delicious apples and almonds.

Level rating

How long? 30 mins prep,
30 mins resting,
40 mins baking

How many? 6–8

• • • • • • • • • • • • • • • • • • •

Ingredients

185g (6½oz) plain flour, plus extra for dusting

¼ tsp salt

1 tsp caster sugar, plus extra for sprinkling

100g (3½oz) unsalted butter, chilled and diced, plus extra for greasing and brushing

1 large egg, beaten

½ tsp cider vinegar

1 tbsp icing sugar, for dusting

For the filling

900g (2lb) tart apples, such as Granny Smith, peeled, cored, and thinly sliced

grated zest of ½ lemon

30g (1oz) breadcrumbs

100g (3½oz) caster sugar

3 tbsp soft dark brown sugar

1 tsp ground cinnamon

¼ tsp grated nutmeg

45g (1½oz) flaked almonds

¼ tsp vanilla extract

1 Combine the flour, salt, and sugar in a large bowl. Rub in 30g (1oz) of the butter until it looks like breadcrumbs. In a separate bowl, whisk the egg, vinegar, and 60ml (2fl oz) cold water. Add the liquid to the dry ingredients and mix to make a loose dough.

2 Knead the dough on a lightly floured work surface for 10-15 minutes until it is smooth and elastic. Put it in a lightly greased bowl, cover with cling film, and leave to rest for 30 minutes.

3 For the filling, combine the apples, zest, breadcrumbs, two types of sugar, cinnamon, nutmeg, almonds, and vanilla in a large bowl. Lightly flour a large, clean, tea towel and place the pastry on top.

START at the CENTRE and WORK OUTWARDS to STRETCH OUT the PASTRY.

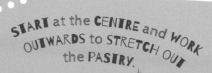

4 Roll the pastry into a large rectangle. Gently stretch it out to about 40 x 61cm (16 x 24in), or until it is very thin. Preheat the oven to 190°C (375°F/Gas 5). Line a baking sheet with baking parchment.

5 Melt the remaining butter in a saucepan over a low heat and brush over the pastry. Put the filling at one end of the pastry. Lift the edges of the tea towel and slowly roll up the strudel, working gently but firmly.

6 Place the strudel on the baking sheet. Curve it into a half circle and brush with melted butter. Sprinkle over some caster sugar and trim the edges. Bake for 35-40 minutes, until golden. Dust with icing sugar and serve warm.

Fruity crumble pie

Topped with a tasty oat and pecan crumble, this pie is sure to be a hit with all your friends. Serve warm with ice cream, or try with salted caramel ice cream for an even richer flavour.

Level rating

How long?   25 mins prep,
30 mins chilling,
1 hr 10 mins baking

How many?   8

Ingredients

For the pastry

200g (7oz) plain flour, plus extra for dusting

100g (3½oz) unsalted butter, chilled and diced, plus extra for greasing

1 egg, beaten

For the topping

75g (2½oz) plain flour

30g (1oz) soft light brown sugar

½ tsp ground cinnamon

75g (2½oz) unsalted butter, softened and diced

45g (1½oz) rolled oats

45g (1½oz) chopped pecans

For the filling

250g (9oz) blueberries

250g (9oz) apples, peeled, cored, and diced into about 1cm (½in) cubes

2 tbsp cornflour

3 tbsp caster sugar

Special equipment

23cm (9in) deep-sided, loose-bottomed fluted tart tin

baking beans

1 Put the flour in a bowl and rub in the butter until it looks like breadcrumbs. Mix in the egg to form a smooth dough. Wrap in cling film and chill for 30 minutes. Preheat the oven to 180°C (350°F/Gas 4). Grease the tin.

2 On a floured surface, roll the pastry into a circle, 5mm (¼in) thick, and use it to line the tin. Trim the excess pastry, prick the base, and line with baking parchment. Fill with baking beans, place on a baking tray and bake for 20 minutes. Take out the beans and paper, and bake for another five minutes. Remove and leave to cool.

3 Increase the oven temperature to 190°C (375°F/Gas 5). For the topping, mix together the flour, sugar, and cinnamon. Rub the butter into the mixture. Stir in the oats and pecans.

4 For the filling, put the blueberries, apples, cornflour and sugar in a bowl. Stir to coat the fruit.

5 Spread the filling evenly in the pastry case and pack it down slightly. Then put the topping on the filling and spread it out loosely and evenly.

Top tip

The apple cubes should be small enough to cook through while baking but not lose their texture.

6 Bake for 40–45 minutes. Cover with foil if it browns too quickly. Cool for 30 minutes. Take out of the tin and serve immediately.

Sweet cherry pie

This pie is popular in America. The fresh cherries and buttery pastry go perfectly together. It is best served warm, with a scoop of vanilla ice cream.

Level rating	
How long?	35 mins prep, 50 mins chilling, 1 hr 5 mins baking
How many?	8

Ingredients

300g (10oz) plain flour, plus extra
   for dusting
1 tsp salt
2 tbsp caster sugar
225g (8oz) unsalted butter, chilled
   and diced
2 tsp apple cider vinegar

For the filling

50g (1¾oz) caster sugar, plus extra
   for sprinkling
30g (1oz) cornflour
1 tbsp lemon juice
grated zest of ½ lemon
pinch of salt
½ tsp vanilla extract
900g (2lb) sweet cherries, pitted
15g (½oz) unsalted butter, chilled
   and diced
1 large egg, lightly beaten, to glaze

Special equipment

23cm (9in) round pie dish,
   about 5cm (2in) deep

1 Put the flour, salt, and sugar in a large bowl and mix well. Rub in the butter until it looks like breadcrumbs. In a separate bowl, mix the vinegar with 180ml (6fl oz) cold water.

2 Slowly add the vinegar mix to the dry ingredients, using two forks to fluff and stir, until well combined.

3 On a lightly floured surface, bring the mixture together to form a loose dough. Knead gently for 4-5 minutes, until soft.

4 Cut off one-third of the dough. Wrap the two portions of dough in cling film and chill for 30 minutes. Grease the pie dish.

5 On a floured surface, roll out the larger portion of the pastry to a 30–33cm (12–13in) circle, about 3mm (⅛in) thick. Use it to line the pie dish, leaving a 2cm (¾in) overhang.

6 For the filling, put the sugar, cornflour, lemon juice, zest, salt, and vanilla in a large bowl and stir to combine. Mix in the cherries and leave to soften for 10–15 minutes.

7 Pour the filling into the pastry and add the butter. Roll out the small portion of pastry to just larger than the pie. Place it on top of the filling and pinch the edges together. Chill in the freezer for 15–20 minutes. Preheat the oven to 200°C (400°F/Gas 6).

8 Brush the top with the beaten egg and sprinkle over the sugar. Cut four slits on top of the pie. Bake for 35–45 minutes, then reduce the temperature to 180°C (350°F/Gas 4). Bake for another 15–20 minutes, until golden.

Pumpkin pie

Dark, rich, and sweet, this American pie has all the fragrance and flavours of autumn, wrapped in a crisp pastry shell. Serve it with a dollop of whipped cream or a scoop of ice cream.

Level rating

How long? 40 mins prep,
1 hr 25 mins baking,
1 hr chilling

How many? 8

Ingredients

115g (4oz) unsalted butter, chilled and diced, plus extra for greasing

150g (5½oz) plain flour, plus extra for dusting

1 tbsp caster sugar

½ tsp salt

1 tsp apple juice

whipped cream, to serve

For the filling

400g (14oz) can pumpkin purée

120ml (4fl oz) whole milk

175g (6oz) soft dark brown sugar

1⅛ tsp ground cinnamon

½ tsp grated nutmeg

⅛ tsp ground allspice

½ tsp salt

2 large eggs

Special equipment

23cm (9in) pie dish, about 5cm (2in) deep
baking beans

1 Grease the pie dish. Mix the flour, sugar, and salt in a bowl. Rub in the butter until the mixture looks like breadcrumbs. In another bowl, mix the apple juice with 120ml (4fl oz) cold water.

2 Add four tablespoons of the liquid mixture to the flour mixture. Use two forks to stir them together until clumps form.

3 On a lightly floured surface, gently knead the mixture until it forms a dough. Wrap in cling film and chill for 30 minutes. Grease the pie dish.

4 On a floured surface, roll out the pastry to a 30cm (12in) circle, 2mm (⅛in) thick. Line the pie dish, leaving a 1cm (½in) overhang. Use your fingers to crimp (pinch) the top of the pie all the way around the edge. Chill for 30 minutes.

5 Preheat the oven to 190°C (375°F/Gas 5).

6 Prick the bottom of the pie with a fork. Line it with baking parchment and fill with baking beans. Place on a baking sheet. Bake for 25 minutes, until lightly brown at the edges.

7 Take out the beans and paper. Bake for 6–10 minutes, until golden. Leave to cool on a wire rack. Reduce the oven temperature to 180°C (350°F/Gas 4).

8 Whisk the pumpkin purée, milk, and brown sugar until smooth. Beat in the spices, salt, and eggs until well mixed.

9 Pour the filling into the pie, and place on a baking sheet. Cover the edges with foil. Bake for 35–40 minutes. Remove the foil and bake for 10 minutes, until set. Serve warm.

Ultimate apple pie

This recipe is one to bake when it's really cold outside. It's a comfort food that all your family and friends will enjoy.

TRY THIS

To make an apple and blackberry pie, add 250g (9oz) blackberries at Step 8 and gently mix together with the apples.

 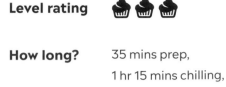
Ingredients

330g (11oz) plain flour, plus extra for dusting

½ tsp salt

150g (5½oz) lard or white vegetable fat, cubed, plus extra for greasing

2 tbsp caster sugar, plus extra for sprinkling

1 tbsp milk, for glazing

For the filling

1kg (2¼lb) eating apples, peeled, cored, and sliced

juice of 1 lemon

2 tbsp plain flour

½ tsp ground cinnamon

¼ tsp grated nutmeg

100g (3½oz) caster sugar

Special equipment

23cm (9in) shallow pie dish

1 Sift the flour and salt into a bowl. Add the lard or vegetable fat and cut across it with two round-bladed knives.

2 Using your fingertips, rub the lard or vegetable fat into the flour until crumbs form. Lift the mixture to add air to it.

3 Add the sugar. Sprinkle with 6–7 tablespoons of cold water. Mix together with a fork.

4 Press the crumbs into a ball, wrap in cling film, and chill for 30 minutes. Grease the dish with lard or vegetable fat.

5 On a floured surface, roll two-thirds of the dough out to a round, 5cm (2in) larger than the dish.

131

6 Using the rolling pin, drape the pastry over the dish and gently push it down.

7 Using a sharp knife, carefully trim any excess pastry, then chill for 15 minutes until firm.

8 Put the apple slices in a bowl and pour on the lemon juice. Mix to coat the apples in juice.

9 Sprinkle the flour, cinnamon, nutmeg, and sugar over the apples. Mix to coat the apples.

10 Put the apples in the dish and use a basting brush to brush the edge of the pastry with water. Roll the rest of the dough to a 28cm (11in) round.

11 Wrap the pastry around the rolling pin and drape it over the filling. Carefully trim the overhang.

12 Press the edges together to seal, carefully crimping with the back of a knife as you go.

13 Carefully cut an "x" in the top crust. Gently pull back the point of each triangle to reveal the filling.

14 Roll out the trimmings, cut into strips, and moisten with a little water. Lay on the pie in a criss-cross pattern. Brush the milk over the pie.

15 Sprinkle over sugar. Chill for 30 minutes. Preheat the oven to 220°C (425°F/Gas 7). Bake for 20 minutes

16 Reduce the oven temperature to 180°C (350°F/Gas 4). Bake for a further 30–35 minutes. Insert a skewer to check the apples are tender. Serve warm.

Very berry plum pie

Berries and plums give this fruity pie a deliciously sweet flavour. It goes perfectly with a scoop of ice cream!

Level rating

How long?   15 mins prep,
30 mins chilling,
30 mins baking

How many?   6–8

Ingredients

plain flour, for dusting

500g (1lb 2oz) ready-prepared puff pastry

1 egg, beaten

650g (1lb 6oz) mixed berries – raspberries
and strawberries

2 tbsp caster sugar

2 tbsp cornflour

200g (7oz) plums, stoned and cut into
quarters

1 On a lightly floured surface, roll out the puff pastry until it's about 5mm (¼in) thick.

2 Put a 25cm (10in) plate on the pastry and carefully cut around it with a knife. Move the circle onto a baking sheet and brush a little beaten egg all over the surface.

3 Mix the berries, sugar, cornflour, and plums together in a large bowl. Gently toss to coat, being careful not to crush the fruit.

4 Spoon the fruit into the middle of the pastry, leaving a 7.5cm (3in) border around the outside.

6 Brush the crust with the remaining beaten egg. Bake for 30 minutes until golden brown, rotating halfway through baking. Leave to cool for 30 minutes, then serve.

5 Scrunch up the edges and bring them towards the centre, leaving the middle uncovered. Chill in the fridge for 30 minutes. Preheat the oven to 200°C (400°F/Gas 6).

SWEET BERRIES

TRY THIS

Other fruits, such as blueberries, peaches, apples, blackberries, and pears will also taste great in this recipe.

Key lime pie

This dessert is named after the small limes that grow in the Florida Keys, US, where the recipe comes from. The zesty limes give the pie a delicious pop of flavour!

Level rating 🧁

How long?   15 mins prep,
                40 mins baking,
                2 hrs chilling

How many?   8

1 Preheat the oven to 180°C (350°F/Gas 4).

2 Pulse the biscuits in a food processor to a fine powder and put in a bowl. Add the butter and mix well to combine.

Ingredients

175g (6oz) digestive biscuits, crushed
75g (2½oz) unsalted butter, melted

For the filling

1 large egg, plus 1 yolk
1 tbsp grated lime zest, plus
    extra to decorate
400g (14oz) can condensed milk
230ml (8fl oz) lime juice
pinch of salt

For the topping

200ml (7fl oz) double cream
2 tsp icing sugar

Special equipment

23cm (9in) round pie dish, about 5cm
    (2in) deep

3 Spread the mixture in the pie dish, pressing it evenly into the bottom and sides for a firm base. Bake for 8–10 minutes, until golden. Set aside to cool.

4 Whisk the egg, yolk, and zest in a bowl for two minutes. Then whisk in the milk, lime juice, and salt until smooth. Pour over the base. Bake for 25–30 minutes, until the filling is set.

5 Leave to cool completely. Chill for two hours. For the topping, beat the cream and sugar in a bowl to form stiff peaks. Spread it over the pie. Decorate with lime zest.

ZINGY AND CREAMY

Top tip

You can store the baked biscuit base in an airtight container in the fridge up to one day ahead of serving.

Raspberry crème tartlets

These tartlets look stunning and are incredibly simple to make. The pastry cases and crème pâtissière are easy to make ahead, so you can assemble the tarts at the last minute.

Level rating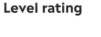

How long?   30 mins prep,
          1½ hrs chilling,
          25 mins baking

How many?   4

Ingredients

175g (6oz) plain flour, plus extra
    for dusting
30g (1oz) caster sugar
100g (3½oz) unsalted butter, chilled
    and diced
1 egg, beaten with 1 tbsp iced water

For the crème pâtissière

250ml (9fl oz) whole milk
2 egg yolks
50g (1¾oz) caster sugar
15g (½oz) cornflour
1 tsp vanilla extract

For the topping

3 tbsp apricot jam, sieved
250g (9oz) raspberries

Special equipment

4 x 10cm (4in) loose-bottomed fluted tart
    tins
baking beans

Top tip

To prepare ahead, store the crème pâtissière in an airtight container in the fridge for up to two days. Wrap and store the pastry cases in the fridge for up to three days.

1 Mix the flour and sugar in a bowl, then rub in the butter to form crumbs. Mix in the egg to make a dough. Add more iced water if it's dry. Knead briefly and wrap in cling film. Chill for 30 minutes.

Trim any EXCESS PASTRY.

2 Preheat the oven to 180°C (350°F/ Gas 4). Divide the pastry into four. On a floured surface, roll out each portion to a circle, 3mm (⅛in) thick, and use to line the tins, leaving an overhang of 1cm (½in).

3 Prick the cases using a fork, line with baking parchment, and fill with baking beans. Bake on a baking tray for 15 minutes. Take out the beans and parchment, and bake for 5–10 minutes. Trim the overhang. Cool completely before taking the pastry cases out of the tins.

4 To make the crème, heat the milk until hot, but not boiling. In a small bowl, whisk the egg yolks, sugar, cornflour, and vanilla, and slowly pour in the hot milk. Put in a saucepan.

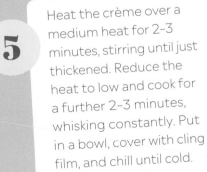

5 Heat the crème over a medium heat for 2–3 minutes, stirring until just thickened. Reduce the heat to low and cook for a further 2–3 minutes, whisking constantly. Put in a bowl, cover with cling film, and chill until cold.

6 Heat the jam and one tablespoon of water over a low heat, stirring until smooth. Take off the heat and let it cool. Spoon the crème pâtissière into the cases. Put the raspberries on top. Add a little apricot glaze. Chill for one hour before serving.

Three ways
with tartlets

These tasty little treats are packed with flavour and are a perfect dessert if you're having friends over. They all taste amazing when served with a bowl of fresh strawberries.

Level rating

How long?
20 mins prep (Custard),
40 mins prep (Banana, Mocha),
30 mins chilling (Banana, Mocha),
20 mins baking (Custard),
45 mins baking (Mocha),
40 mins baking (Banana)

How many?
6 (Custard),
4 (Banana, Mocha)

Custard tartlets

Ingredients

25g (scant 1oz) unsalted butter
3 sheets filo pastry
flour, for dusting

For the filling
225ml (7½fl oz) whole milk
150ml (5fl oz) double cream
6 cardamom pods, crushed
2 eggs, whisked
25g (scant 1oz) caster sugar

Special equipment
deep 6-hole, 6cm (2½in) wide muffin tin,
    greased

1 Preheat the oven to 190°C (375°F/Gas 5).

2 Heat the milk, cream, and cardamom pods in a heavy-based saucepan until steaming. Take off the heat.

3 Melt the butter in a separate saucepan over a medium heat.

4 On a floured surface, spread out one filo pastry sheet and brush it with a little of the melted butter.

5 Cover with another pastry sheet, brush with butter, and top with the final pastry sheet. Cut the pastry into six equal pieces.

6 Line the tin with the pastry, allowing the edges to stick up over the rim. Brush the edges with butter. Cover with a damp paper towel.

7 Combine the eggs and sugar in a bowl. Pour the milk through a sieve into the egg mix. Whisk the custard, transfer to a jug, and pour evenly into the pastry cases.

8 Bake for 15–20 minutes. Cool in the tin for 10 minutes, then remove.

Banana and chocolate tartlets

Ingredients

175g (6oz) plain flour
25g (scant 1oz) caster sugar
100g (3½oz) unsalted butter, chilled
1 egg yolk

For the filling and topping

10g (¼oz) desiccated coconut
25g (scant 1oz) plain flour
25g (scant 1oz) soft light brown sugar
25g (scant 1oz) unsalted butter, softened
2–3 bananas, cut into 1cm (½in) slices
6 tbsp chocolate spread

Special equipment

6 x 10cm (4in) loose-bottomed tart tins
baking beans

1 Follow the instructions for Steps 1–3 on page 139. Then, increase the oven temperature to 200°C (400°F/Gas 6).

2 In a bowl, combine the coconut, flour, and brown sugar. Rub in the butter, until the mixture looks like breadcrumbs.

3 Line each pastry case with banana slices and one tablespoon of chocolate spread. Sprinkle over the coconut topping loosely.

4 Bake for 15 minutes. Leave to cool in the tins, then remove and serve.

Mocha tartlets

Ingredients

125g (4½oz) plain flour
30g (1oz) caster sugar
30g (1oz) cocoa powder
100g (3½oz) unsalted butter, chilled and diced
3 tbsp cooled strong black coffee

For the filling

300ml (10fl oz) double cream
250g (9oz) dark chocolate, chopped
2 eggs
1 tsp vanilla extract

Special equipment

6 x 10cm (4in) loose-bottomed tart tins
baking beans

1 Combine the flour, sugar, and cocoa in a bowl. Rub in the butter, until the mixture looks like breadcrumbs.

2 Add the coffee. Bring together to form a dough. Knead it briefly until smooth, wrap in cling film, and chill for 30 minutes.

3 Follow Steps 2 and 3 on page 139. Then reduce the oven temperature to 160°C (325°F/Gas 3).

4 Heat the double cream in a heavy-based saucepan until steaming. Remove and stir in the chocolate, until melted. Beat until smooth, move to a bowl, and leave to cool.

5 Gradually whisk in the eggs and stir in the vanilla. Pour the filling into the tart cases.

6 Bake for 20 minutes. Leave to cool in the tins. Then remove and serve immediately.

Tangy lemon tart

This French tart, known as "tarte au citron", is filled to the brim with mouthwatering lemony custard. Serve this delicious dessert with single cream and raspberries.

Level rating   🧁 🧁

How long?   20 mins prep,
1 hr chilling,
1 hr 10 mins baking

How many?   8

Ingredients

200g (7oz) plain flour, plus extra
for dusting
30g (1oz) caster sugar
100g (3½oz) unsalted butter,
chilled and diced
1 egg, beaten
single cream, to serve
raspberries, to serve

For the filling

200ml (7fl oz) double cream
200g (7oz) caster sugar
grated zest and juice of 2 lemons
4 eggs, plus 1 egg yolk

Special equipment

23cm (9in) loose-bottomed fluted tart tin
baking beans

1 Mix the flour and sugar in a bowl. Then rub in the butter to form crumbs. Stir in the egg to form a dough. Add a little iced water if dry. Knead briefly on a floured surface, until smooth. Wrap in cling film and chill for one hour.

2 Preheat the oven to 180°C (350°F/Gas 4). On a floured surface, roll out the pastry to a large circle, 3mm (⅛in) thick. Use it to line the tin, leaving an overhang of 2cm (¾in). Knead the pastry briefly if it crumbles. Prick the pastry, line with baking parchment, and fill with baking beans.

3 Place on a baking sheet and bake for 20–25 minutes. Remove the beans and parchment, and bake for another five minutes, until golden. Trim the pastry. For the filling, whisk all the ingredients in a bowl until well combined.

4 Pour the filling into the pastry case. Bake on a baking tray for 40–45 minutes, until just set. Take out of the tin, and cool to room temperature before serving.

Chocolate tart

With its deliciously rich filling, this tart is perfect for chocoholics. It can be served warm or cold and goes perfectly with fresh raspberries.

Level rating

How long?   30 mins prep,
                1 hr chilling,
                40 mins baking

How many?   8–10

Ingredients

150g (5½oz) plain flour, plus extra for dusting
100g (3½oz) unsalted butter, chilled and diced
50g (1¾oz) caster sugar
1 egg yolk
½ tsp vanilla extract
raspberries, to serve

For the filling

150g (5½oz) unsalted butter, diced
200g (7oz) good-quality dark chocolate, broken into pieces
3 eggs
30g (1oz) caster sugar
100ml (3½fl oz) double cream

Special equipment

22cm (9in) loose-bottomed fluted tart tin
baking beans

1 In a large bowl, rub the flour and butter together until fine crumbs form.

2 Add the sugar to the crumb mixture and stir to combine.

3 Beat the egg yolk with the vanilla, then add them to the crumb mixture.

4 Bring it together to form a dough. Add a little cold water if it is dry. Wrap in cling film and chill for one hour.

5 Preheat the oven to 180°C (350°F/Gas 4). On a floured surface, roll out the pastry to a circle, 3mm (⅛in) thick.

6 If the pastry begins to crumble, bring it together with your hands and knead gently. Then roll it out again.

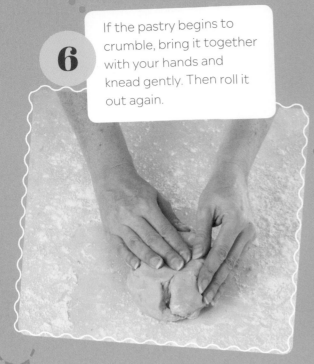

7 Use it to line the tart tin, leaving an overlapping edge of 2cm (¾in). With a pair of scissors, carefully trim any excess pastry that hangs down further than this.

8 Prick the pastry base all over with a fork to prevent air bubbles forming during baking.

9 Line the pastry case with baking parchment. Scatter baking beans over and put the tin on a baking sheet. Bake for 20 minutes.

Top tip

The tart will keep in the fridge for up to two days.

10 Remove the beans and parchment. Bake for five minutes more. Trim any excess pastry.

11 Melt the butter and chocolate in a heatproof bowl over a pan of simmering water, stirring. Set aside to cool.

12 Whisk together the eggs and caster sugar in a bowl until well blended.

13 Pour in the cooled chocolate mixture and whisk gently until well combined.

14 Mix in the double cream. Pour the chocolate mixture into a jug.

15 Keeping the pastry case on the baking sheet, pour the filling into the pastry case and smooth the top.

16 Bake for 10–15 minutes until just set. Leave to cool for five minutes, then remove from the tin and place on a serving plate.

Pinwheel pear tart

Rich, buttery pastry makes this French tart irresistible. The combination of pears and frangipane (a sweet almond paste) is absolutely delicious. You could use apples instead of pears if you prefer.

Ingredients

75g (2½oz) unsalted butter, softened and diced, plus extra for greasing

175g (6oz) plain flour, sifted, plus extra for dusting

3 egg yolks

60g (2oz) caster sugar

pinch of salt

½ tsp vanilla extract

3–4 ripe pears, peeled, cored, and cut into wedges

juice of 1 lemon

double cream, to serve

For the frangipane

125g (4½oz) unsalted butter, softened

100g (3½oz) caster sugar

1 egg, plus 1 egg yolk, lightly beaten

125g (4½oz) ground almonds

2 tbsp plain flour, sifted

For the glaze

150g (5½oz) apricot jam

Special equipment

23cm (9in) loose-bottomed, fluted tart tin

1 Grease the tart tin. Put the flour in a large bowl and make a well in the centre. Put the butter, egg yolks, sugar, salt, and vanilla extract in the well and mix to combine.

2 Use your fingertips to bring the mix together and make a sticky dough. Add cold water if needed. Lightly knead the dough on a floured surface for 1–2 minutes. Wrap in cling film. Chill for 30 minutes.

3 On a floured surface, roll out the pastry to a 28cm (11in) circle. Line the tin and trim any overhang. Prick the base with a fork and chill for 15 minutes.

4

Preheat the oven to 200°C (400°F/Gas 6).

5

For the frangipane, beat the butter and sugar in a large bowl for 2–3 minutes, until fluffy. Beat in the egg and yolk, a little at a time. Stir in one tablespoon of water, the ground almonds, and flour.

6

Coat the pears with the lemon juice in a small bowl. Spread the frangipane evenly in the tart case and top with the pears in a spiral pattern. Put the tin on a baking sheet and bake for 12–15 minutes. Reduce the heat to 180°C (350°F/Gas 4). Bake for a further 25–30 minutes, until the filling is set.

7

Cool slightly, then take out of the tin. For the glaze, push the jam through a sieve into a heatproof bowl. Add 2–3 tablespoons of water, melt over a saucepan of hot water, and brush over the tart. Serve warm, with double cream.

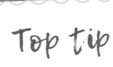

Top tip

You can prepare and store the tart case in an airtight container in the fridge for up to three days ahead of serving.

Almond and raspberry lattice tart

Pastry is easy to make patterns with, and it creates an impressive dessert. In this recipe it's used to make a criss-cross design.

Level rating

How long? 35 mins prep,
2 hrs chilling,
45 mins baking

How many? 6–8

Ingredients

125g (4½oz) plain flour,
 plus extra for dusting
pinch of ground cloves
½ tsp ground cinnamon
175g (6oz) ground almonds
125g (4½oz) unsalted butter, softened
 and diced, plus extra for greasing
1 egg yolk
100g (3½oz) caster sugar
¼ tsp salt
finely grated zest of 1 lemon and juice
 of ½ lemon

For the filling

125g (4½oz) caster sugar
375g (13oz) raspberries
1–2 tbsp icing sugar, for dusting

Special equipment

23cm (9in) loose-bottomed fluted tart tin
fluted pastry wheel (optional)

1 Sift the flour into a bowl. Mix in the cloves, cinnamon, and almonds, and make a well.

2 Using your fingers, mix the butter, yolk, sugar, salt, zest, and juice in a separate bowl. Place in the well.

3 Mix in the flour with your fingers and work it until coarse crumbs form. Form the dough into a ball.

4 Knead the dough for 1–2 minutes until smooth. Wrap in cling film. Chill for 1–2 hours.

5 Cook the caster sugar and raspberries in a pan for 10–12 minutes until thick. Leave to cool.

6 With the back of a wooden spoon, press half of the fruit pulp through a sieve.

7 Stir in the remaining pulp from the pan. Grease the tin and preheat the oven to 190°C (375°F/Gas 5).

8 Flour the work surface. Roll out two-thirds of the dough into a 28cm (11in) round.

9 Use the dough to line the tin, and cut off any excess overhang.

Top tip

The tart can be stored in an airtight container for up to two days.

10 Spread the filling in the case. Roll the rest of the dough to a 15 x 30cm (6 x 12in) rectangle.

11 Using a fluted wheel, for a decorative edge, cut the dough into 12 x 1cm (5 x ½in) strips.

12 Arrange half the strips from left to right over the tart, 2cm (¾in) apart.

13 Put the other strips diagonally over. Trim the overhang, roll out the trimmings, and cut four strips.

14 Brush the edge of the pastry with water and fix on the edge strips. Chill for 15 minutes.

15 Bake for 15 minutes. Reduce the oven temperature to 180°C (350°F/Gas 4) and bake for 25–30 minutes more.

16 Leave to cool, then remove from the tin and, about 30 minutes before serving, lightly dust with icing sugar.

Strawberry tart

This gorgeous tart tastes as good as it looks. Finished with a jelly glaze, it will look as if it were made by a professional pastry chef!

Top tip

The tart is best eaten on the day it's made, but will keep chilled overnight.

Ingredients

150g (5½oz) plain flour, plus extra
  for dusting
100g (3½oz) unsalted butter, chilled
  and diced
50g (1¾oz) caster sugar
1 egg yolk
½ tsp vanilla extract
6 tbsp redcurrant jelly, for glazing
300g (10oz) strawberries, hulled, washed
  and thickly sliced

For the crème pâtissière

100g (3½oz) caster sugar
50g (1¾oz) cornflour
2 eggs
1 tsp vanilla extract
400ml (14fl oz) whole milk

Special equipment

22cm (9in) loose-bottomed fluted tart tin
baking beans

1 In a bowl, rub the flour and butter together to form fine crumbs. Stir in the sugar.

2 Beat together the egg yolk and vanilla extract, and add to the flour mixture.

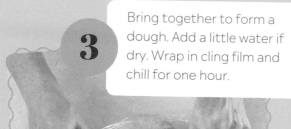

3 Bring together to form a dough. Add a little water if dry. Wrap in cling film and chill for one hour.

4 Preheat the oven to 180°C (350°F/Gas 4). Roll out the pastry to a thickness of 3mm (⅛in).

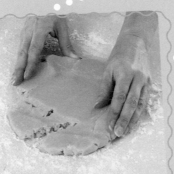

5 If the pastry starts to crumble, bring it together with your hands and gently knead.

6 Use the rolled-out pastry to line the tin, leaving an overlapping edge of 2cm (¾in) around the tin.

7 Use a pair of scissors or a knife to trim any excess pastry that hangs down further than 2cm (¾in).

8 Prick the pastry base all over with a fork, to prevent air bubbles forming as it bakes.

9 Carefully line the pastry case with a piece of baking parchment.

10 Scatter the baking beans over the parchment. Put on a baking sheet and bake for 20 minutes.

11 Take out the beans and parchment, and bake for five minutes more. Carefully trim any excess pastry with a knife.

12 Melt the jelly with one tablespoon of water and brush a little over the pastry case. Leave to cool.

13 For the crème pâtissière, beat the sugar, cornflour, eggs, and vanilla extract in a bowl.

14 In a heavy-based saucepan, bring the milk to the boil and take it off the heat just as it bubbles.

15 Pour the hot milk onto the egg mixture, whisking all the time.

16 Put the mixture back in the pan and bring to the boil over a medium heat, whisking continuously.

17 When the crème thickens, reduce the heat to low, and continue to cook for 2–3 minutes, still whisking.

18 Move to a bowl, cover with cling film and leave it to cool completely.

19 Beat the crème pâtissière and spread it over the pastry case. Top with the strawberries, arranging them in circles.

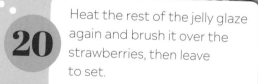

20 Heat the rest of the jelly glaze again and brush it over the strawberries, then leave to set.

21 Remove from the tin to serve.

Apple crumble

Crumble is a traditional English dessert and it tastes great served with cream, ice cream, or custard.

Level rating

How long?   20 mins prep,
40 mins baking

How many?   6–8

Ingredients

25g (scant 1oz) butter, cubed

900g (2lb) Bramley apples, peeled, cored and sliced into wedges

50g (1¾oz) demerara sugar

2 tbsp apple juice

For the topping

100g (3½oz) plain flour

75g (2½oz) butter, cubed

125g (4½oz) rolled jumbo oats

50g (1¾oz) demerara sugar

4 tbsp mixed seeds, such as sunflower and pumpkin

1 tsp ground cinnamon

double cream, ice cream, or custard, to serve

Special equipment

1 litre (1¾ pints) baking dish

1

Preheat the oven to 180°C (350°F/Gas 4).

2

Melt the butter in a pan and stir in the apples, sugar, and apple juice.

3

Cook for 5–6 minutes, covered, then spoon the apple mixture into the baking dish.

4

For the topping, put the flour in a bowl and rub in the butter with your fingertips until the mixture looks like breadcrumbs. Stir in the oats, sugar, seeds, and cinnamon.

5

Spoon the mixture evenly over the top of the apples. Bake for 30–40 minutes, until the topping is golden. Serve warm.

Three ways
with crumble

Follow the instructions on pages 158–159 to make the crumbly topping for all of these delicious crumbles. Try out your own variations, such as swapping the oats for the same quantity of flour for a smoother crumble.

Level rating

How long?
20 mins prep,
50 mins baking (Autumn fruits),
40 mins baking (Cherry, Plum)

How many?
6–8

Autumn fruits crumble

Ingredients

60g (2oz) walnuts
½ tsp ground cinnamon
2 heaped tbsp soft light brown sugar
4–5 eating apples, peeled, cored, and cut into cubes
2–3 pears, peeled, cored, and cut into cubes
100g (3½oz) cranberries
1 heaped tbsp plain flour
crumble topping (see pages 158–159)
double cream or ice cream, to serve

Serve with **CREAM** or **ICE CREAM**.

1 Preheat the oven to 180°C (350°F/Gas 4). Bake the walnuts for five minutes on a baking tray. Leave to cool, then chop into small pieces.

2 Mix the walnuts, cinnamon, sugar, fruit, and flour together in an oven dish.

3 Pack it all down gently and then sprinkle the crumble topping evenly over the fruit filling. Bake for 45–50 minutes. Serve warm.

Cherry crumble

Ingredients

550g (1¼lb) stoned cherries
2 tbsp caster sugar
2 tbsp apple juice
crumble topping (see pages 158–159)
custard, to serve

1 Preheat the oven to 180°C (350°F/Gas 4).

2 Place the cherries in an oven dish, scatter over the sugar and drizzle over the apple juice. Sprinkle the crumble topping over evenly.

3 Bake for 35–40 minutes or until golden brown. Serve warm.

Plum crumble

Ingredients

600g (1lb 5oz) plums, stoned and halved
2 tbsp maple syrup or honey, to drizzle
crumble topping (see pages 158–159)
custard, to serve

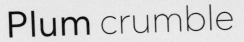

Serve with **CUSTARD.**

TRY THIS
For the topping, swap the plain flour for wholemeal flour to give the crumble a nuttier flavour.

1 Preheat the oven to 180°C (350°F/Gas 4).

2 Place the plums in an oven dish, drizzle over the maple syrup or honey, and sprinkle the crumble topping over evenly.

3 Bake for 30–40 minutes or until the top is golden brown and the plum juices are bubbling. Serve warm.

Tomato and onion tarts

When cooked, puff pastry rises and leaves air pockets inside, making it light and fluffy. Although light, these tarts are surprisingly filling.

Ingredients

plain flour, for dusting

375g (13oz) ready-prepared puff pastry

oil, for greasing

250g (9oz) cherry tomatoes

250g (9oz) ricotta cheese

2 eggs, beaten

2 tbsp freshly chopped basil

25g (scant 1oz) Parmesan or mozzarella
    cheese, grated

salt and freshly ground black pepper

1 red onion, sliced

basil leaves, to garnish

TRY THIS

To make this a sweet tart,
swap the tomatoes for
strawberries and the
cheese with chocolate.
Take out the red onion,
seasoning, and fresh basil.

162

1 Preheat the oven to 200°C (400°F/Gas 6).

2 On a lightly floured surface roll out the pastry into a rectangle measuring 25 x 38cm (10 x 15in).

3 Use a knife to cut six equal squares of pastry, then score a 1cm (½in) border around the edges. Move the squares onto a greased baking tray.

4 Carefully slice the cherry tomatoes in half, using a sharp knife.

5 In a large mixing bowl, mix the ricotta, eggs, basil, and Parmesan cheese. Season with salt and pepper.

6 Spread the mixture on the squares, making sure to stay inside the borders. Scatter the tomatoes and red onion on top and bake for 20 minutes, or until golden. Sprinkle the basil leaves over the tarts before serving.

Mini spinach and filo tarts

These simple and light tarts are easy to make for an afternoon snack or for a birthday party. Filo pastry is tricky to make from scratch, so buy it ready-made.

Level rating

How long? 15 mins prep,
25 mins baking

How many? 8

Ingredients

1 tbsp olive oil, plus extra for greasing

250g (9oz) baby spinach leaves, washed

2 tbsp fresh basil

250g (9oz) cream cheese

1 medium egg, beaten

25g (scant 1oz) Cheddar or Parmesan
cheese, grated

salt and freshly ground black pepper

250g (9oz) filo pastry

Special equipment

2 x 6-hole or 1 x 12-hole muffin tins

1 Preheat the oven to 180°C (350°F/Gas 4). Brush the muffin tins with oil and set aside. Tear the spinach and the basil leaves into pieces.

2 In a large mixing bowl, beat the cream cheese, egg, and grated cheese until smooth. Season with salt and pepper, then stir in the spinach and basil.

3 Carefully cut the filo pastry into 16 squares measuring 12.5cm (5in). Brush the squares with a little olive oil.

TRY THIS

To make this into a meaty version, sprinkle 50g (1¾oz) cooked and chopped bacon over the tops of the tarts before baking.

CREAMY AND CRISPY

4

Place one square on top of another pastry square at an angle to make a star shape. Repeat this process with the rest of the pastry sheets to make eight tarts.

5

Gently place the pastry sheets in the muffin tins. Push them into the corners to make them fit.

6

Spoon the mixture into the casings and smooth it down with the back of the spoon. Bake the tarts for 25 minutes until the filling has set. Serve warm.

Cheesy veggie tart

This savoury tart is packed with a delicious creamy filling and is perfect for lunch or a picnic. If you can't find Swiss chard, try adding spinach instead.

Level rating	
How long?	30 mins prep, 1 hr chilling, 1 hr 10 mins baking
How many?	6–8

Ingredients

150g (5½oz) plain flour, plus extra for dusting
75g (2½oz) unsalted butter, chilled and diced
1 egg yolk

For the filling

1 tbsp olive oil
1 onion, finely chopped
sea salt
2 garlic cloves, finely chopped
few sprigs of fresh rosemary, leaves picked and finely chopped
250g (9oz) Swiss chard, roughly chopped
125g (4½oz) Gruyère cheese, grated
125g (4½oz) feta cheese, cubed
freshly ground black pepper
2 eggs, lightly beaten
200ml (7fl oz) double cream or whipping cream

Special equipment

22cm (9in) loose-bottomed fluted tart tin
baking beans

166

1 To make the pastry, rub the flour and butter together in a bowl until fine crumbs form.

2 Lightly beat the egg yolk with one tablespoon of cold water.

3 Add the yolk mix to the crumbs and bring together to form a soft dough. Add extra water if it is too dry.

4 Wrap the dough in cling film and chill for one hour. Preheat the oven to 180°C (350°F/Gas 4).

5 On a floured work surface, roll the pastry out to a large circle, about 3mm (⅛in) thick.

6 Use the rolling pin to carefully lift the pastry and put it into the tin, leaving a 2cm (¾in) overhang.

Gently push the pastry into the tin with your fingers. Prick the bottom all over with a fork. **7**

8 Line with baking parchment and fill with baking beans. Put the pastry case on a baking sheet.

Bake for 20–25 minutes. Remove the beans and parchment. Bake for five more minutes. Leave to cool and carefully trim the edges with a knife. **9**

Top tip

The tart is best eaten the same day, but can be chilled overnight if baking in advance.

Heat the oil in a pan over a low heat. Add the onion and a pinch of salt. Fry the onion until soft. Add the garlic and rosemary, and cook for a few seconds. **10**

11 Add the Swiss chard to the pan. Stir for about five minutes until it wilts.

12 Keeping the pastry case on the baking sheet, spoon in the onion and chard mixture.

13 Sprinkle over the Gruyère cheese and scatter with the feta. Season well with salt and pepper.

14 Using a fork, mix together the eggs and cream in a jug until well combined. Carefully pour the cream mix over the tart filling. Bake for 30–40 minutes until golden.

15 Leave to cool, then remove from the tin and move to a serving dish. Serve warm or at room temperature.

Mighty meat pie

This is wonderful to take on a picnic, served with chutney and a crisp green salad.

Level rating

How long? 1 hr prep, 30 mins chilling, 1½ hrs baking

How many? 8–10

Ingredients

500g (1lb 2oz) plain flour, plus extra for dusting
2 tsp salt
75g (2½oz) butter, chilled and diced, plus extra for greasing
75g (2½oz) lard, chilled and diced

For the filling

9 eggs
4 skinless, boneless chicken breasts, total weight 750g (1lb 10oz)
375g (13oz) lean boneless pork
finely grated zest of ½ lemon
1 tsp dried thyme
1 tsp dried sage
large pinch of ground nutmeg
pinch of sea salt and freshly ground black pepper
375g (13oz) cooked lean ham

Special equipment

20–23cm (8–9in) springform cake tin
mincer or food processor with blade attachment

Top tip

The pie will keep in the fridge for up to three days.

1

Sift the flour and salt into a large bowl. Rub in the butter and lard until fine crumbs form.

2

Make a well in the flour and add 150ml (5fl oz) of cold water. Stir the mixture with a knife to form coarse crumbs.

3

Using your hands, form a dough and knead until smooth. Wrap in cling film and chill for 30 minutes.

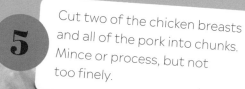

4

In a pan, put six eggs in water, bring to the boil, and simmer for seven minutes. Drain, cool, and peel the egg shells off.

5

Cut two of the chicken breasts and all of the pork into chunks. Mince or process, but not too finely.

6

Put the minced meats in a large bowl. Add the lemon zest, thyme, sage, nutmeg, salt, and pepper.

7 In a separate bowl, whisk two eggs and add to the minced meats. Beat the filling until it pulls away from the sides of the bowl.

8 Cut the leftover chicken breasts and the ham into 2cm (¾in) cubes, and stir into the filling.

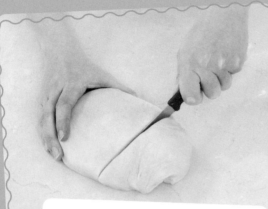

9 Grease the tin. Shape about three-quarters of the dough into a ball. Keep the rest covered with cling film.

10 On a floured surface, roll the dough out to the size of the tin, with a 2.5cm (1in) overhang. Place it in the tin.

11 Preheat the oven to 200°C (400°F/Gas 6). Spoon in half the filling and put the boiled eggs on top.

12 Gently push in the eggs and cover with the remaining mix. Fold over the overhang.

13 Beat the last egg with a pinch of salt, and brush the edges of the pastry with the egg glaze.

14 Roll out the remaining dough to 5mm (¼in) thick. Lay on top, press to seal, and trim the edges.

15 Poke a hole in the lid. Roll a piece of foil into a tube and place in the hole. The foil creates a chimney, allowing steam to escape from the pie while it is baking.

16 Cut out strips, 2.5cm (1in) wide from the dough trimmings, and cut them into leaf shapes. Mark the veins with a knife.

17 Arrange the leaves in a circle, glaze, and bake for one hour. Reduce the oven temperature to 180°C (350°F/Gas 4) and bake for another 30 minutes.

18 Discard the foil chimney and leave to cool before taking the pie out of the tin. Serve at room temperature.

Cornish pasties

Invented in Cornwall, England, by mine workers, the traditional crusty handle (rippled top) prevented miners from getting their food grubby. Now we can eat the whole pasty!

Level rating

How long? 20 mins prep,
1 hr chilling,
45 mins baking

How many? 4

TRY THIS

For a veggie option, use grated Cheddar cheese instead of beef skirt. Omit the Worcestershire sauce and use vegetable shortening instead of lard.

Top tip

These will keep in the fridge for up to two days.

Ingredients

100g (3½oz) lard, chilled and diced
50g (1¾oz) unsalted butter, chilled and diced
300g (10oz) plain flour, plus extra for dusting
½ tsp salt
1 egg, beaten, for glazing

For the filling

250g (9oz) beef skirt, trimmed, cut into 1cm (½in) cubes
80g (2¾oz) swede, peeled, and cut into 5mm (¼in) cubes
100g (3½oz) waxy potatoes, peeled, and cut into 5mm (¼in) cubes
1 large onion, finely chopped
splash of Worcestershire sauce
1 tsp plain flour
sea salt and freshly ground black pepper

1 Rub the lard and butter into the flour in a bowl, until it forms fine crumbs. Add the salt and enough cold water to bring the mixture together to make a soft dough.

2 Knead the dough briefly on a lightly floured surface. Wrap in cling film and chill for one hour. Preheat the oven to 190°C (375°F/Gas 5).

3 Mix all the filling ingredients together in a bowl and season well.

4 On a floured work surface, roll the pastry out to a thickness of 5mm (¼in). Using a small plate, cut four circles.

5 Fold the circles in half, then open them out again, leaving a slight fold down the centre.

6 Pile one-quarter of the filling into each circle, leaving a 2cm (¾in) border all around. Brush the border of the pastry with the egg.

7 Pull both edges up over the filling and press together to seal. Crimp the sealed edge with your fingers. Brush the egg over the pasties. Bake for 40–45 minutes on a baking tray, until golden. Cool for 15 minutes before eating.

CLEVER COOKIES AND TEATIME TREATS

Bake scrumptious traybakes, cookies, and shortbreads. Then exercise your meringue-whipping muscles to create perfect pavlovas and marvellous macarons.

Clever cookies

By adding a few different ingredients to this basic cookie dough, you can have a variety of tasty treats. Turn to pages 180–181 to see the extras you can add.

Ingredients

100g (3½oz) butter, softened

125g (4½oz) caster sugar

1 egg

½ tsp vanilla extract

150g (5½oz) self-raising flour

see pages 180–181 for the extra ingredients to add to the cookie dough

1

Preheat the oven to 180°C (350°F/Gas 4).

2

Line two baking sheets with baking parchment.

3

Cream the butter and sugar together in a bowl with an electric whisk, then beat in the egg and vanilla extract.

4

Using a metal spoon, stir in the flour and any extra ingredients (see pages 180–181) and mix together.

5

Roll the dough into 16 balls and place on the baking sheets, leaving a little space around them. Flatten slightly and bake for 12-15 minutes.

Four ways with cookies

Try out these tasty combinations or come up with your own cookie flavours. Make a batch and wrap them up as a present.

Level rating

How long?
10 mins prep,
15 mins baking

How many?
16

Chocolate chunks

Ingredients

Extras to add to dough recipe
75g (2½oz) dark chocolate chunks or chocolate chips
75g (2½oz) white chocolate chunks or chocolate chips

Follow the steps on page 179, and add these ingredients at Step 4.

Cinnamon and raisin

Ingredients

Extras to add to dough recipe
1 tsp ground cinnamon
125g (4½oz) raisins

Follow the steps on page 179, and add these ingredients at Step 4.

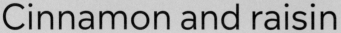

Lemon and blueberry

Ingredients

Extras to add to dough recipe

2 tsp grated lemon zest

100g (3½oz) blueberries

Follow the steps on page 179, and add these ingredients at Step 4.

White chocolate and cranberry

Ingredients

Extras to add to dough recipe

100g (3½oz) white chocolate chunks or chocolate chips

75g (2½oz) dried cranberries

Which **cookie** will **you** choose?

Follow the steps on page 179, and add these ingredients at Step 4.

Cheesy nutty biscuits

These crunchy savoury biscuits are delicious served warm or cold. Serve them for lunch or a snack with your favourite cheese and some salad or relish.

Level rating

How long?   10 mins prep,
1 hr chilling,
20 mins baking

How many?   24

Ingredients

120g (4¼oz) Stilton cheese, or other
   blue cheese
50g (1¾oz) unsalted butter, softened
125g (4½oz) plain flour, sifted, plus extra
   for dusting
60g (2oz) walnuts, chopped
freshly ground black pepper
1 egg yolk

Special equipment

5cm (2in) round pastry cutter

1 Mix the cheese and butter together in a bowl with an electric whisk until soft and creamy.

2 Add the flour to the cheese mixture and rub it in with your fingertips to form crumbs.

3 Stir in the walnuts and a grinding of black pepper. Add the egg yolk and bring the mixture together to form a stiff dough.

4 Knead the dough briefly on a lightly floured work surface. Wrap it in cling film and chill for one hour. Preheat the oven to 180°C (350°F/Gas 4).

5 Turn the dough out onto a floured work surface and knead it briefly to soften slightly. Roll it out to a thickness of 5mm (¼in) and cut out the biscuits with the pastry cutter.

6 Put the rounds on non-stick baking sheets and bake for 15 minutes. Turn them over and bake for another five minutes until golden brown. Let them cool a little on their sheets, then move to a wire rack to cool completely, or serve warm.

Hazelnut and raisin oat biscuits

These crunchy and chewy biscuits are a slightly healthier alternative to chocolate chip cookies. They're perfect to take along on a picnic.

Level rating

How long? 20 mins prep, 15 mins baking

How many? 18

Ingredients

100g (3½oz) hazelnuts

100g (3½oz) unsalted butter, softened

200g (7oz) soft light brown sugar

1 egg, beaten

1 tsp vanilla extract

1 tbsp runny honey

125g (4½oz) self-raising flour, sifted

125g (4½oz) jumbo porridge oats

pinch of salt

100g (3½oz) raisins

a little milk, if needed

1 Preheat the oven to 190°C (375°F/Gas 5). Toast the hazelnuts in the oven on a baking sheet for five minutes.

2 Once toasted, rub with a clean tea towel to remove most of the skins.

3 Roughly chop the hazelnuts and then set aside.

4 Cream together the butter and sugar with an electric whisk until smooth.

5 Add the egg, vanilla extract, and honey, and beat again until smooth.

6 Combine the flour, oats, and salt in a separate bowl, and stir to mix.

7 Stir the flour mix into the creamed mixture and beat until well combined.

8 Add the chopped nuts and raisins, and mix until evenly distributed.

9 If the mixture is too stiff, add a little milk until it is easier to work with.

10 Line two or three baking sheets with baking parchment. Roll the dough into 18 small balls.

11 Place the balls on the baking sheets and flatten them slightly, leaving plenty of space between them.

12 Bake for 10-15 minutes, until golden. Move to a wire rack to cool.

Top tip

The cookies will keep in an airtight container for up to five days.

Butter biscuits

These deliciously buttery biscuits are quick and simple to make, leaving you plenty of time for the fun part – eating them!

Ingredients

100g (3½oz) caster sugar

225g (8oz) plain flour, sifted, plus extra for dusting

150g (5½oz) unsalted butter, softened and diced

1 egg yolk

1 tsp vanilla extract

Special equipment

7cm (2¾in) round pastry cutter

TRY THIS

When the biscuits are completely cooled, try dipping them in 175g (6oz) melted dark, milk, or white chocolate.

Top tip

The biscuits will keep in an airtight container for up to five days.

1

Preheat the oven to 180°C (350°F/Gas 4).

2

Put the sugar, flour, and butter into a large bowl and rub them together until the mixture looks like fine breadcrumbs.

3

Add the egg yolk and vanilla extract, and bring the mixture together into a dough. Put the dough onto a lightly floured work surface and knead it briefly until smooth.

4

Flour the dough and work surface well, and roll the dough out to a thickness of about 5mm (¼in). If it is too sticky, chill it for 15 minutes, then try again.

5

Use the pastry cutter to cut out the biscuits and put them on two or three non-stick baking sheets. Re-roll the pastry offcuts and cut out biscuits until all the dough is used.

6

Bake for 10–15 minutes until golden brown. Leave the biscuits to cool until just firm, then move to a wire rack to cool completely.

Shortbread biscuits

A Scottish classic, this shortbread is deliciously sweet and buttery – perfect for sharing with your friends and family.

Level rating

How long?   15 mins prep,
1 hr chilling,
40 mins baking

How many?   8

Ingredients

150g (5½oz) unsalted butter, softened,
   plus extra for greasing
75g (2½oz) caster sugar,
   plus extra for sprinkling
175g (6oz) plain flour
50g (1¾oz) cornflour

Special equipment

18cm (7in) loose-bottomed round cake tin

1 Grease the tin and line the base and sides with baking parchment.

2 Put the softened butter and sugar in a large bowl.

3 Cream together the butter and sugar with an electric whisk until light and fluffy.

4 Stir in the flour and cornflour very gently, stopping as soon as the flours are mixed in.

5 Bring the mixture together with your hands to form a very rough, crumbly dough. Put in the tin.

6 Firmly push the dough down with your hands to form a compact, even layer.

7 With a sharp knife, carefully score the circle of shortbread into eight wedges.

8 Prick the shortbread all over with a fork to make a decorative pattern.

9 Cover with cling film. Chill for one hour. Preheat the oven to 160°C (325°F/Gas 3).

10 Bake for 30–40 minutes. Cover with foil if it browns quickly.

11 Take the shortbread out of the oven, and carefully re-score the wedges with a sharp knife.

12 While still warm, sprinkle a thin layer of caster sugar evenly over the top. When cooled, turn out of the tin and cut into wedges along the scored lines.

Gingerbread biscuits

This recipe is quick to make and the dough is really easy to handle. Use different cookie cutters if you want to make other shapes.

Ingredients

4 tbsp golden syrup

300g (10oz) plain flour, plus extra
    for dusting

1 tsp bicarbonate of soda

1½ tsp ground ginger

1½ tsp mixed spice

100g (3½oz) unsalted butter, softened
    and diced

150g (5½oz) soft dark brown sugar

1 egg

raisins, to decorate

75g (2½oz) icing sugar, sifted (optional)

Special equipment

11cm (4½in) gingerbread man cutter
piping bag with thin nozzle (optional)

1 Preheat the oven to 190°C (375°F/Gas 5). Heat the golden syrup until it melts, then cool.

2 Sift the flour, bicarbonate of soda, and spices into a bowl. Add the butter and rub together with your fingertips to form fine crumbs.

3 Add the sugar to the flour mixture and mix well.

4 Beat the egg into the cooled syrup until well blended.

5 Make a well in the flour mixture. Pour in the syrup mix. Bring together to form a rough dough.

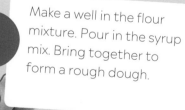

6 On a lightly floured work surface, knead the dough briefly until smooth.

7 Flour the dough and the work surface well, and roll the dough out to a thickness of 5mm (¼in). Using the cutter, cut out as many shapes as possible. Put on non-stick baking sheets.

8 Decorate the biscuits with raisins, giving them eyes, a nose, and buttons down the front.

9 Bake for 10–12 minutes, until golden. Put on a wire rack to cool completely.

10 If using, mix the icing sugar in a bowl with enough water to form the icing. Put the icing in the piping bag.

Top tip
These gingerbread biscuits will keep in an airtight container for up to three days.

11 Decorate the biscuits with the piped icing to resemble clothes, hair, or whatever you prefer.

12 Leave the icing to set completely before serving or storing.

Gingerbread house

This beautiful gingerbread house is the perfect wintry centrepiece. Trace the templates from the end of this book to get the shapes just right.

Level rating

How long? 30 mins prep,
13 mins baking,
1 day assembling

How many? 8

Ingredients

175ml (6fl oz) golden syrup
115g (4oz) unsalted butter, plus extra
for greasing
115g (4oz) soft dark brown sugar
600g (1lb 5oz) plain flour, sifted,
plus extra for dusting
1 tsp ground cinnamon
4 tsp ground ginger
4 tsp bicarbonate of soda, dissolved
in 4 tsp cold water
2 egg yolks

For the icing

3 egg whites
1 tsp lemon juice, plus extra if needed
700g (1¾lb) icing sugar, sifted
red colouring paste (optional)

Special equipment

traced templates from the end of this book
(photocopy the templates, enlarging them
by 200 per cent, and cut them out)
tree-shape cookie cutters

1 Melt the syrup, butter, and sugar in a saucepan. In a large bowl, sift together the flour, cinnamon, and ginger. Make a well in the centre.

2 Stir in the soda mix, yolks, and melted syrup mix. Knead into a dough on a floured surface. Preheat the oven to 180°C (350°F/Gas 4). Lightly grease and line a baking tray.

3 Roll out the dough to a thickness of 5mm (¼in). Put the templates on the dough and cut around them carefully using a sharp knife.

Festive treat

4 Roll out the dough trimmings and cut out tree shapes. Put all the pieces on the tray. Bake for 10–13 minutes, until firm and just beginning to brown at the edges. Trim any rough edges with a sharp, hot knife.

5 Using an electric whisk, beat the egg whites in a large bowl. Stir in the lemon juice. Gradually add the icing sugar.

6 Beat until the icing is smooth and paste-like. Add extra juice if it's too thick. Put one tablespoon aside and colour it red.

7 Once the gingerbread pieces are cool, pipe your designs before you assemble.

8 To assemble, work on the board that the gingerbread house will be presented on. Start from the bottom upwards, applying icing to the joins with a palette knife.

9 Allow each join to dry. Make sure the base is dry before you attach the roof. Hold the roof in place for a few minutes. Once dry, pipe it with the icing to create snow and icicles.

Be inventive with **YOUR DESIGN.**

Set the scene with **THE EXTRA BISCUITS.**

French shortbread

These all-butter French treats are called *sablés*, or "sandy", due to their delicious crumbly texture. Use them to sandwich ice cream, as shown here, dip them in chocolate, or enjoy them on their own.

Level rating

How long? 30 mins prep, 15 mins chilling, 45 mins baking

How many? 30

Ingredients

225g (8oz) plain flour, plus extra for dusting

100g (3½oz) caster sugar

150g (5½oz) unsalted butter, softened and diced

1 egg yolk

1 tsp vanilla extract

vanilla ice cream, to serve

blueberries, to serve

Special equipment

7cm (2¾in) round pastry cutter

Top tip

You can prepare and store the dough, wrapped in the fridge, up to three days ahead. Or freeze it up to three months ahead.

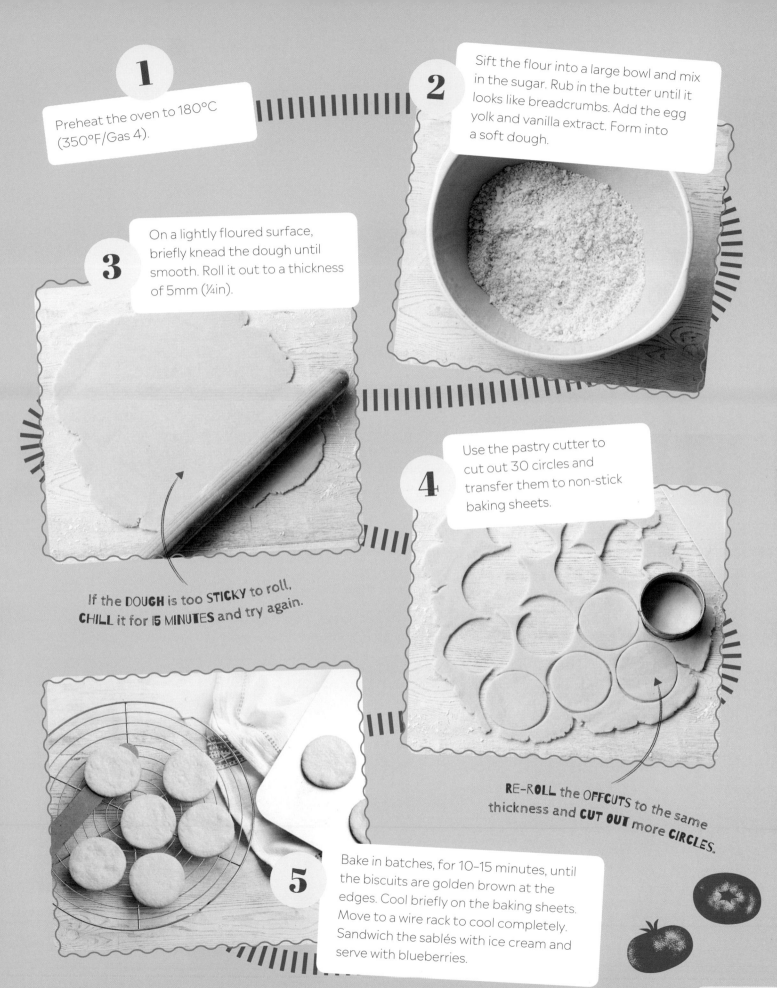

1

Preheat the oven to 180°C (350°F/Gas 4).

2

Sift the flour into a large bowl and mix in the sugar. Rub in the butter until it looks like breadcrumbs. Add the egg yolk and vanilla extract. Form into a soft dough.

3

On a lightly floured surface, briefly knead the dough until smooth. Roll it out to a thickness of 5mm (¼in).

If the DOUGH is too STICKY to roll, CHILL it for 15 MINUTES and try again.

4

Use the pastry cutter to cut out 30 circles and transfer them to non-stick baking sheets.

RE-ROLL the OFFCUTS to the same thickness and CUT OUT more CIRCLES.

5

Bake in batches, for 10–15 minutes, until the biscuits are golden brown at the edges. Cool briefly on the baking sheets. Move to a wire rack to cool completely. Sandwich the sablés with ice cream and serve with blueberries.

Granola bars

These chunky treats are great for breakfast or as a quick snack. The peanut butter and dates make them really soft and chewy!

Level rating

How long? 15 mins prep,
24 mins baking

How many? 16

Ingredients

vegetable oil, for greasing
250g (9oz) rolled oats
100g (3½oz) almonds, roughly chopped
75g (2½oz) mixed seeds, such as sunflower,
   pumpkin, and sesame
100g (3½oz) runny honey
125g (4½oz) crunchy peanut butter
100g (3½oz) pitted dates
100g (3½oz) dried mixed berries, such
   as blueberries, cherries, cranberries,
   and raisins

Special equipment

28 x 18cm (11 x 7in) baking tray
food processor

Store any leftover BARS in an AIRTIGHT container.

1

Preheat the oven to 180°C (350°F/Gas 4).

2

Lightly oil the tray and add the oats, almonds, and seeds. Bake for 10–12 minutes.

3

Warm the honey and peanut butter in a pan over a low heat. Stir occasionally, until combined.

Allow to **COOL** slightly, then **CUT INTO BARS** and leave to **SET** in the tin.

4

Put the dates, four tablespoons of warm water, and the honey mixture in a food processor, and blend until smooth.

5

Mix the date and oat mixtures in a bowl with the berries and stir until combined. Spoon into a tin and flatten with the back of a spoon. Bake for 12 minutes.

CLASSIC CRUSTS

Roll up your sleeves and get ready
to master a variety of loaves,
flatbreads, rolls, and baguettes.
Refer to the technique pages at
the beginning of this book
for tips on how to make the
best bread ever!

8 Knead for 10 minutes until it is very smooth, elastic, and makes a ball.

9 Grease a large bowl with butter. Put in the dough and flip it to butter the surface lightly.

10 Cover with a damp tea towel. Leave it in a warm place for 1–1½ hours, until doubled in size.

11 Grease two baking sheets. Place the dough on a floured work surface and knock it back.

12 Cover and let it rest for five minutes. Cut it into three equal pieces, then cut one piece in half.

13 Cover one large and one small piece of dough with a tea towel, and shape the rest.

14 Shape one large piece into a loose ball. Fold in the sides, turn, and pinch to make a tight ball.

15 Put the ball, seam side down, onto the baking sheet.

16 Similarly, shape one small piece into a ball. Set it, seam side down, on top of the first ball.

17 Using your forefinger, press through the centre of the balls down to the baking sheet.

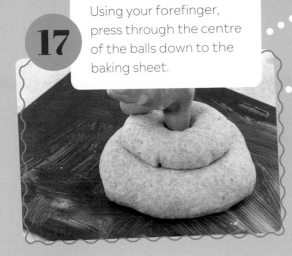

18 Repeat with the remaining two dough balls, to shape a second loaf.

19 Cover both loaves with tea towels. Leave in a warm place for 45 minutes or until doubled in size.

20 Preheat the oven to 190°C (375°F/Gas 5). Bake for 40-45 minutes until well browned.

21 The loaves should sound hollow when tapped on the base. Cool on a wire rack.

Rye bread

This crusty German loaf is more chewy and has a stronger flavour than bread made from wheat flour.

Level rating

How long? 40 mins prep, 2 hrs 45 mins rising and proving, 55 mins baking

How many? 1 loaf

1 Put the dissolved yeast, treacle, two-thirds of the caraway seeds, salt, and oil into a bowl.

2 Pour in the sparkling water. Stir in the rye flour, and mix together well with your hands.

3 Gradually add the strong white flour until it forms a soft, slightly sticky dough.

Ingredients

2½ tsp dried yeast, dissolved in 4 tbsp lukewarm water

1 tbsp black treacle

1 tbsp caraway seeds

2 tsp salt

1 tbsp vegetable oil, plus extra for greasing

250ml (9fl oz) sparkling water

250g (9oz) rye flour

175g (6oz) very strong white bread flour, plus extra for dusting

polenta (fine yellow cornmeal), for dusting

1 egg white, beaten until frothy, for glazing

4 Knead for 8–10 minutes on a floured surface, until smooth and elastic, and put in an oiled bowl.

5 Cover with a damp tea towel. Put in a warm place for 1½–2 hours until doubled in size.

6 Sprinkle a baking sheet with polenta. Knock back the dough on a floured work surface.

8 Roll it back and forth on the work surface, putting pressure on the ends to make them narrower.

7 Cover with cling film and let it rest for five minutes. Pat the dough into an oval, about 25cm (10in) long.

9 Put on a baking sheet. Cover with cling film and leave in a warm place for 45 minutes, until doubled in size.

10 Preheat the oven to 190°C (375°F/Gas 5). Brush the beaten egg over the loaf to glaze.

11 Sprinkle with the remaining caraway seeds and press them into the dough.

12 Carefully make three diagonal slashes, about 5mm (¼in) deep, on top. Bake for 50-55 minutes. Put on a wire rack to cool.

Ciabatta

The name "ciabatta" is the Italian word for slipper! A good ciabatta should be well risen and crusty, with large air pockets.

Level rating

How long?   30 mins prep, 3 hrs rising and proving, 30 mins baking

How many?   2 loaves

Ingredients

2 tsp dried yeast
2 tbsp olive oil, plus extra for greasing
450g (1lb) strong white bread flour, plus extra for dusting
1 tsp sea salt

1 Dissolve the yeast in 350ml (12fl oz) lukewarm water, then add the oil.

2 Put the flour and salt in a bowl. Make a well, pour in the yeast, and stir to form a soft dough.

3 Knead on a floured surface for 10 minutes until smooth and soft.

4 Put the dough in a lightly oiled bowl and cover loosely with cling film.

5 Leave to rise in a warm place for two hours until doubled in size. Turn out onto a floured surface.

6 Gently knock back the dough, then divide it into two equal pieces.

7 Knead them briefly and shape into long rectangles, around 30 x 10cm (12 x 4in).

8 Place each loaf on a lined baking sheet, with enough space to allow it to expand.

9 Cover loosely with cling film and a tea towel. Leave for one hour until doubled in size.

10 Preheat the oven to 230°C (450°F/Gas 8). Spray the loaves with a fine mist of water.

11 Bake for 30 minutes, spraying them with water every 10 minutes.

12 It is cooked when the top is golden brown and the base sounds hollow when you tap it.

Top tip

These are best eaten the same day, but can be stored overnight, wrapped in paper.

Easy bread rolls

These rolls are easy to make and fun to shape. They are great served with butter or loaded with your favourite sandwich filling.

Level rating

How long? 55 mins prep,
2 hrs rising and proving,
18 mins baking

How many? 16

Ingredients

150ml (5fl oz) milk
60g (2oz) unsalted butter, cubed,
   plus extra for greasing
2 tbsp caster sugar
3 tsp dried yeast
2 eggs, plus 1 yolk, for glazing
2 tsp salt
550g (1¼lb) strong white bread flour,
   plus extra for dusting
poppy seeds, for sprinkling

1 Bring the milk to a boil. Put four tablespoons into a small bowl and let it cool to lukewarm. Add the butter and sugar to the remaining milk in the pan and stir until melted. Cool to lukewarm.

2 Sprinkle the yeast over the four tablespoons of milk. Leave for five minutes to dissolve. Stir once. In a large bowl, lightly beat the eggs. Add the sweetened milk, salt, and dissolved yeast.

3 Gradually stir in the flour until the dough forms a ball. It should be soft and slightly sticky.

4 Knead the dough on a floured work surface for 5–7 minutes until smooth and elastic. Put in a greased bowl. Cover with cling film. Put in a warm place for 1–1½ hours until doubled in size.

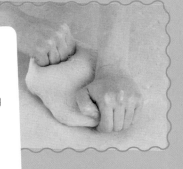

6 Cut in half, and roll each piece into a cylinder. Cut each cylinder into eight equal pieces.

5 Line two baking sheets with baking parchment. On a floured work surface, knock back the dough.

7 To shape round rolls, roll the dough in a circular motion so it forms a smooth ball.

8 For a baker's knot, roll the dough into a rope, shape into an eight, and tuck the ends through the holes.

9 For a snail shape, roll the dough into a long rope and wind it around in a spiral, tucking the end underneath.

10 Put the rolls on the baking sheets. Cover with a tea towel. Leave in a warm place for 30 minutes.

11 Preheat the oven to 220°C (425°F/Gas 7). Beat the egg yolk with a tablespoon of water.

12 Brush all the rolls with the egg. Sprinkle the poppy seeds on the round rolls. Bake for 15–18 minutes until golden brown.

SERVE WARM

Baguette

To create a light and soft baguette you first need to make a "sponge" which is a starter dough that rises for 12 hours. Then you add it to the other ingredients to make a delicious bread.

Level rating

How long? 30 mins prep,
12 hrs or overnight fermenting, 3½ hrs rising and proving,
20 mins baking

How many? 2 loaves

Ingredients

For the sponge

⅛ tsp dried yeast
75g (2½oz) strong white or brown
    bread flour
1 tbsp rye flour
vegetable oil, for greasing

For the dough

1 tsp dried yeast
300g (10½oz) strong white or brown
    bread flour, plus extra for dusting
½ tsp salt

1 For the sponge, dissolve the yeast in 75ml (2½fl oz) lukewarm water and add to the two types of flour.

2 Form a sticky, loose dough and place in an oiled bowl, with room for it to expand.

3 Cover with cling film and put in a cool place to rise for at least 12 hours.

4 To make the dough, dissolve the yeast in 150ml (5fl oz) lukewarm water, whisking continuously.

5 Put the risen sponge, flour, and salt into a large bowl and pour in the yeast liquid.

6 Stir it all together with a wooden spoon to form a soft dough.

7 Knead for 10 minutes on a floured surface until smooth, glossy, and elastic.

8 Put in an oiled bowl, cover with cling film, and leave to rise in a warm place for two hours.

9 Put it on a floured surface. Knock it back. Carefully divide into two equal portions.

10 Knead briefly and shape each piece into a rectangle. Tuck one short edge into the centre.

11 Press down firmly, fold over the other short edge, and press firmly again.

12 Shape the dough into a rounded oblong. Pinch to seal and turn seam side down.

13 Shape into a long, thin log shape that is 4cm (1½in) in wide.

14 Place the loaves on baking trays and cover with oiled cling film and a clean tea towel.

15 Keep in a warm place for 1½ hours until doubled in size. Preheat the oven to 220°C (425°F/Gas 7).

16 Carefully slash each loaf deeply on the diagonal along the top.

17 Dust with a little flour, spray with water, and put the loaves in the oven.

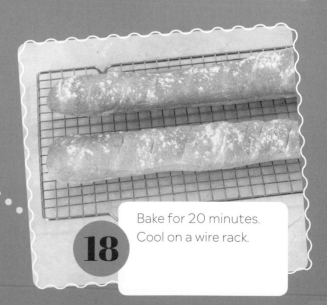

18 Bake for 20 minutes. Cool on a wire rack.

Bagels

These soft and springy bagels are perfect for breakfast or lunchtime – slice them open and spread with butter, or sandwich together with a filling of your choice.

Level rating   🧁🧁

How long?   40 mins prep,
3 hrs rising and proving,
20–25 mins baking

How many?   8–10

Ingredients

600g (1lb 5oz) strong white bread flour, plus extra for dusting

2 tsp fine salt

2 tsp caster sugar

2 tsp dried yeast

1 tbsp sunflower oil, plus extra for greasing

1 egg, beaten, for glazing

1 Put the flour, salt, and sugar in a bowl. In a separate bowl, mix the yeast with 300ml (10fl oz) lukewarm water.

2 Add the oil to the yeast, mix and pour the liquid into the flour mixture, stirring together to form a soft dough.

3 Knead on a floured surface for 10 minutes, until smooth. Put in an oiled bowl. Cover with cling film and leave in a warm place for 1–2 hours, until doubled in size.

4 Put the dough on a floured surface, press it down to its original size, and divide into 8–10 pieces.

5 Take each piece of dough and roll it under your palm to make a fat log shape.

6 Using your palms, continue to roll it towards each end, until it is about 25cm (10in) long.

7 Take the dough and wrap it around your knuckles, so the join is on your palm.

8 Squeeze gently together, then roll briefly to seal the join. The hole should still be big at this stage. Repeat to shape all the bagels.

9 Line two baking sheets with baking parchment and put the bagels on the trays. Cover with cling film and a tea towel. Leave in a warm place for up to one hour, until doubled in size.

10 Preheat the oven to 220°C (425°F/Gas 7). Boil a large pan of water, then let it simmer. Cook the bagels in the water for one minute on either side.

11 Remove them from the water with a slotted spoon. Dry them briefly on a clean tea towel. Return the bagels to the baking sheets and brush them with the beaten egg.

12 Bake in the centre of the oven for 20–25 minutes, until golden. Cool for at least five minutes on a wire rack before serving.

Pretzels

These traditional German breads are surprisingly easy to make. Have fun plaiting the dough to create the unique pretzel shape.

Level rating

How long? 50 mins prep,
1½–2½ hrs rising and
proving, 20 mins baking

How many? 16

Ingredients

350g (12oz) strong white bread flour, plus
    extra for dusting
150g (5½oz) plain flour
1 tsp salt
2 tbsp caster sugar
2 tsp dried yeast
1 tbsp sunflower oil, plus extra
    for greasing

For the glaze

¼ tsp bicarbonate of soda
coarse sea salt or 2 tbsp sesame seeds
1 egg, beaten, for glazing

1 Put the two types of flour, salt, and sugar into a large bowl.

2 Sprinkle the yeast over 300ml (10fl oz) lukewarm water. Stir, leave for five minutes, and add the oil.

3 Gradually pour the liquid into the flour mixture, stirring to form a soft dough.

4 Knead for 10 minutes until smooth and soft. Transfer to an oiled bowl.

5 Cover loosely with cling film and leave in a warm place for 1–2 hours, until nearly doubled in size.

6 Turn the dough out onto a lightly floured work surface, and gently knock it back.

7 With a sharp knife, carefully cut the dough neatly into 16 equal pieces.

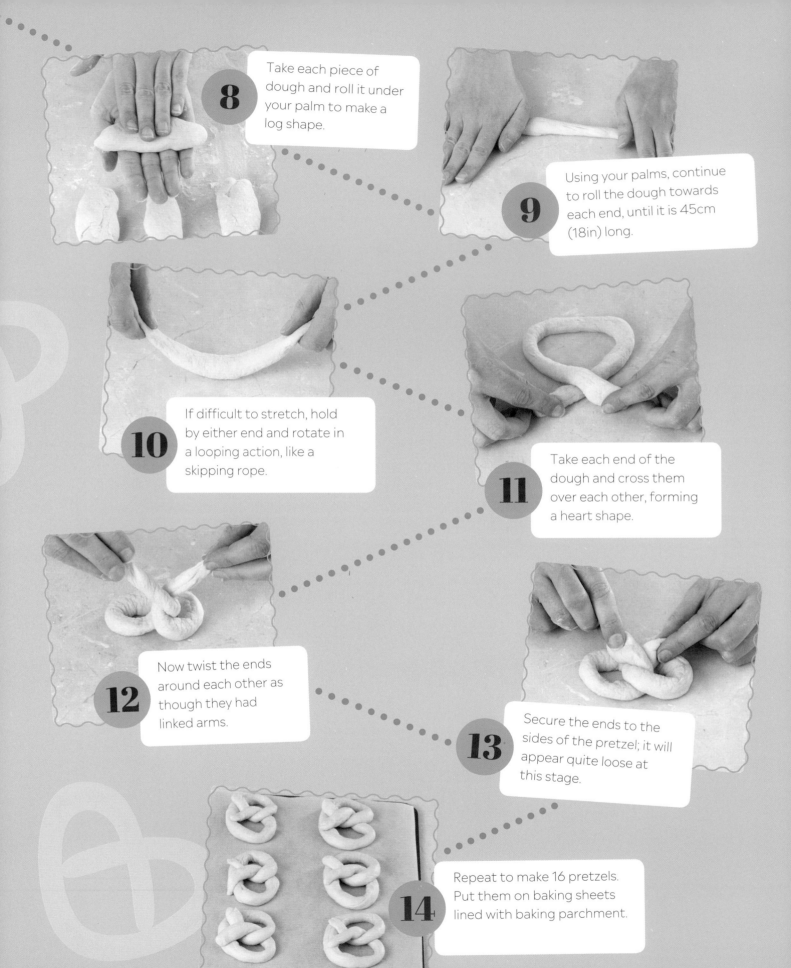

8 Take each piece of dough and roll it under your palm to make a log shape.

9 Using your palms, continue to roll the dough towards each end, until it is 45cm (18in) long.

10 If difficult to stretch, hold by either end and rotate in a looping action, like a skipping rope.

11 Take each end of the dough and cross them over each other, forming a heart shape.

12 Now twist the ends around each other as though they had linked arms.

13 Secure the ends to the sides of the pretzel; it will appear quite loose at this stage.

14 Repeat to make 16 pretzels. Put them on baking sheets lined with baking parchment.

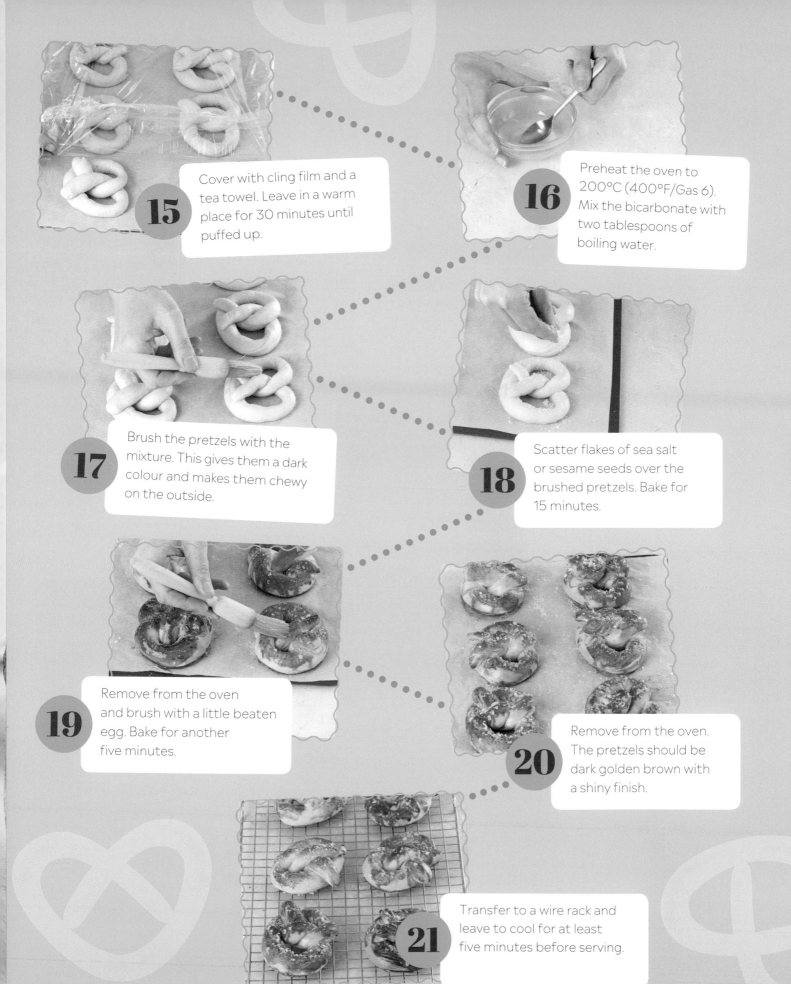

15 Cover with cling film and a tea towel. Leave in a warm place for 30 minutes until puffed up.

16 Preheat the oven to 200°C (400°F/Gas 6). Mix the bicarbonate with two tablespoons of boiling water.

17 Brush the pretzels with the mixture. This gives them a dark colour and makes them chewy on the outside.

18 Scatter flakes of sea salt or sesame seeds over the brushed pretzels. Bake for 15 minutes.

19 Remove from the oven and brush with a little beaten egg. Bake for another five minutes.

20 Remove from the oven. The pretzels should be dark golden brown with a shiny finish.

21 Transfer to a wire rack and leave to cool for at least five minutes before serving.

Four seasons pizza

This tasty pizza has four different toppings all at once! You can prepare the sauce a day ahead and leave the dough to rise overnight, to quickly assemble the next day.

Level rating

How long?   40 mins prep,
1½ hrs rising,
20 mins baking

How many?   4

1   Mix the flour and salt. In a separate bowl, dissolve the yeast in 360ml (12fl oz) tepid water. Add the oil to the yeast mix, then combine with the flour to form a dough.

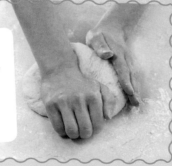

2   Knead on a floured surface for 10 minutes, or until the dough is smooth and elastic.

3   Roll the dough into a ball and place in an oiled bowl. Cover with oiled cling film. Leave in a warm place for 1–1½ hours, until doubled in size, or store in the fridge overnight.

4   For the sauce, put a pan over a low heat. Add the butter, shallots, oil, bay leaf, and garlic. Stir and cover for 5–6 minutes, stirring occasionally.

Ingredients

500g (1lb 2oz) strong white bread flour, plus extra for dusting

½ tsp salt

3 tsp dried yeast

2 tbsp olive oil, plus extra for greasing

For the tomato sauce

25g (scant 1oz) unsalted butter

2 shallots, finely chopped

1 tbsp olive oil

1 bay leaf

3 garlic cloves, crushed

1kg (2¼lb) ripe plum tomatoes, deseeded and chopped

2 tbsp tomato purée

1 tbsp caster sugar

sea salt and freshly ground black pepper

For the toppings

175g (6oz) mozzarella cheese, drained and thinly sliced

115g (4oz) mushrooms, thinly sliced

2 tbsp extra virgin olive oil

2 roasted red peppers, thinly sliced

8 anchovy fillets, halved lengthways

115g (4oz) pepperoni, thinly sliced

2 tbsp capers

8 artichoke hearts, halved

12 black olives

Special equipment

4 baking sheets or pizza trays

5 Add the tomatoes, purée, and sugar. Cook for five minutes, whilst stirring. Pour in 250ml (9fl oz) water, bring to the boil, and reduce the heat to a simmer.

6 Cook for 30 minutes, stirring, until it forms a thick sauce. Season with salt and pepper. Using a wooden spoon, press the sauce through a sieve. Cover and chill until needed.

7 Preheat the oven to 200°C (400°F/Gas 6). Put the dough on a floured surface. Knead lightly, divide into four, and roll or press out into 23cm (9in) rounds.

8 Grease the baking sheets and carefully lift the pizza bases onto each sheet. Spread the sauce over the bases, leaving a 2cm (¾in) border around the edges.

9 Top the pizzas with the mozzarella. Arrange the mushroom slices on a quarter of each pizza and brush with the olive oil.

10 Pile the roasted pepper slices on another quarter with the anchovy fillets on top. Use pepperoni and capers for the third, and artichokes and olives for the fourth quarter.

11 Bake, two at a time, for 15–20 minutes, or until the topping is golden and the base is crispy. Serve hot.

Two ways
with pizza

Have a pizza party with these delicious pizzas! Bianca is covered in a creamy white sauce instead of tomato, and Calzone is a folded pizza with a tasty surprise inside.

Level rating

How long?
25 mins prep,
1½ hrs rising (Bianca),
2 hrs rising (Calzone),
20 mins baking

How many?
4

Pizza bianca

Ingredients

500g (1lb 2oz) strong white bread flour, plus extra for dusting
½ tsp salt
3 tsp dried yeast
2 tbsp olive oil, plus extra for greasing

For the topping
4 tbsp extra virgin olive oil
140g (5oz) Gorgonzola cheese, crumbled
12 slices Parma ham, torn into strips
4 fresh figs, each cut into 8 wedges, and peeled
2 tomatoes, deseeded and diced
115g (4oz) wild rocket leaves
freshly ground black pepper

1 To make the dough, follow Steps 1, 2, 3, and 7 on pages 250–251. Divide the dough into four portions. Preheat the oven to 200°C (400°F/Gas 6).

2 Brush the pizzas with half the olive oil and scatter the cheese over the surface. Bake for 20 minutes or until the bases are crisp.

3 Remove from the oven. Arrange the ham, figs, and tomatoes on top. Return to the oven for another eight minutes or until the toppings are just warmed and the bases are golden brown.

4 Scatter over the rocket, season with plenty of black pepper, and serve at once, drizzled with the rest of the olive oil.

Calzone

Ingredients

500g (1lb 2oz) strong white bread flour,
   plus extra for dusting
½ tsp salt
3 tsp dried yeast
2 tbsp olive oil, plus extra for greasing

For the filling
4 tbsp extra virgin olive oil, plus extra to serve
2 onions, thinly sliced
2 red peppers, cored and cut into strips
1 green pepper, cored and cut into strips
1 yellow pepper, cored and cut into strips
3 garlic cloves, finely chopped
1 small bunch of any herb, such as rosemary,
   thyme, basil, or parsley, or a mixture,
   finely chopped
sea salt
cayenne pepper, to taste
175g (6oz) mozzarella cheese, drained
   and sliced
1 egg, beaten, for glazing
½ tsp salt

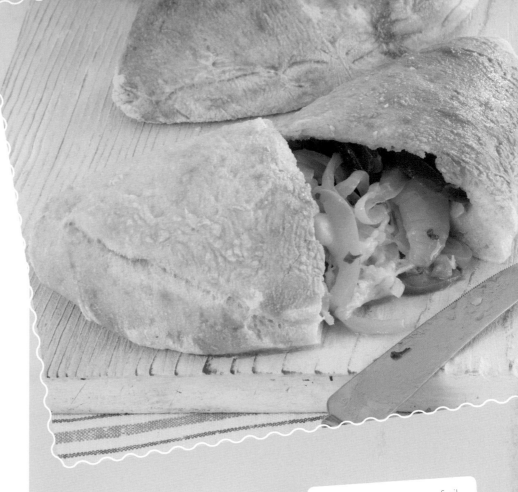

1 To make the dough, follow Steps 1, 2, and 3 on page 250.

2 Heat one tablespoon of oil in a pan and add the onions. Cook for five minutes until soft but not brown. Put in a bowl and set aside.

3 Add the remaining oil to the pan with the peppers, garlic, and herbs. Season with sea salt and cayenne pepper. Fry for 7–10 minutes, stirring, until soft but not brown. Add to the onions, and let it cool.

4 Move the dough to a floured surface. Knead lightly, divide into four, and then roll and pull each piece into a square 1cm (½in) thick.

5 Spoon the pepper mixture onto a diagonal half of each square, leaving a 2.5cm (1in) border.

6 Put the mozzarella on top. Wet the edge of each square with water, and fold one corner over to meet the other, forming a triangle. Pinch the edges together. Put on a floured baking sheet. Leave to rise in a warm place for 30 minutes.

7 Preheat the oven to 230°C (450°F/Gas 8). Whisk the egg with the salt and brush over the calzones. Bake for 15–20 minutes, until golden brown. Brush with a little olive oil before serving.

Pitta bread

This pocket bread is delicious stuffed with salad and other fillings, or cut up and eaten with dips.

Level rating

How long? 30 mins prep,
1 hr 50 mins rising
and proving,
5 mins baking

How many? 6

Ingredients

1 tsp dried yeast

60g (2oz) strong wholemeal bread flour

250g (9oz) strong white bread flour,
plus extra for dusting

1 tsp salt

2 tsp cumin seeds

2 tsp olive oil, plus extra for greasing

1 In a bowl, mix the yeast with four tablespoons of lukewarm water. Leave for five minutes, then stir.

2 In a large bowl, mix together the two types of flour, salt, and cumin seeds. Make a well and pour in the yeast mix, 190ml (6¾fl oz) lukewarm water, and oil.

3 Using a spoon, combine the ingredients to form a soft, sticky dough. Put on a floured surface.

4 Knead until smooth and elastic. Put the dough in a lightly greased bowl and cover with a damp tea towel. Leave to rise in a warm place for 1–1½ hours, until doubled in size.

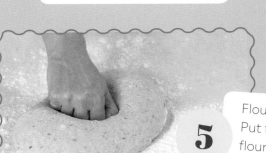

5 Flour two baking sheets. Put the dough on a lightly floured surface, and knock it back.

6 Shape the dough into a cylinder 5cm (2in) wide, then carefully cut into six equal pieces.

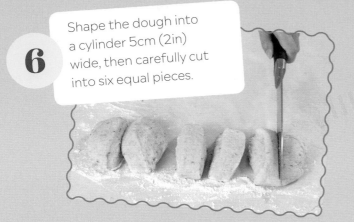

7 Take one piece of dough and leave the rest covered with a tea towel as you work. Shape the dough into a ball, then roll into an 18cm (7in) oval. Repeat with the remaining dough.

8 Transfer three pittas to a baking sheet. Cover with a tea towel. Leave in a warm place for 20 minutes and preheat the oven to 240°C (475°F/Gas 9).

9 Place the other baking sheet in the oven. Once hot, put the three pittas on the sheet and bake for five minutes.

10 Move to a wire rack and brush the tops lightly with water. Bake the remaining pittas, move to the rack, and brush with water. Let the bread cool before serving.

Naan bread

This traditional Indian flatbread goes perfectly with curry and is delicious when served warm.

Level rating 🧁🧁

How long? 20 mins prep, 1 hr rising, 8 mins baking, 1 min grilling

How many? 6

Ingredients

50g (1¾oz) ghee or unsalted butter

500g (1lb 2oz) strong white bread flour, plus extra for dusting

2 tsp dried yeast

1 tsp caster sugar

1 tsp salt

2 tsp black onion (nigella) seeds

100ml (3½fl oz) full-fat plain yogurt

1 Heat the ghee or butter in a small saucepan until melted. Take off the heat.

2 In a large bowl, mix together the flour, yeast, sugar, salt, and onion seeds.

3 Make a well. Add 200ml (7fl oz) lukewarm water, the yogurt, and the melted ghee or butter.

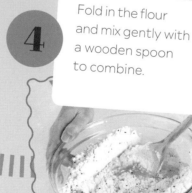

4 Fold in the flour and mix gently with a wooden spoon to combine.

5 Keep mixing for five minutes until it forms a rough dough.

6 Cover with cling film and keep in a warm place for about one hour, until doubled in size. Preheat the oven to 240°C (475°F/Gas 9).

7 Put three baking sheets in the oven. Knock back the dough.

9 Roll each piece into an oval shape about 24cm (10in) long. Remove the baking trays from the oven.

8 Knead the dough on a floured surface until smooth. Divide into six equal pieces.

TRY THIS
For garlic and coriander naan, add 2 crushed garlic cloves and 4 tablespoons finely chopped coriander in Step 2.

11 Preheat the grill to its hottest setting. Move the bread to the grill pan.

10 Put the bread on the preheated sheets and bake for 6–7 minutes, until well puffed.

12 Grill the naans for 30 seconds on each side or until they brown and blister. Move to a wire rack.

Top tip
When grilling, take care not to put the breads too close to the heat, to prevent burning.

Two ways with naan bread

Try stuffing simple naan bread dough with this herby feta mix for a tasty picnic dish, or make peshwari naans for a sweeter flavour.

Level rating

How long?
15 mins prep,
1 hr rising,
6–7 mins baking

How many?
6

Feta, chilli, and herb-stuffed naan bread

Ingredients

500g (1lb 2oz) strong white bread flour, plus extra for dusting
2 tsp dried yeast
1 tsp caster sugar
1 tsp salt
2 tsp black onion (nigella) seeds
100ml (3½fl oz) full-fat plain yogurt
50g (1¾oz) ghee or butter, melted

For the filling
150g (5½oz) feta cheese, crumbled
1 tbsp finely chopped red chilli
3 tbsp chopped mint
3 tbsp chopped coriander

1 Mix the flour, yeast, sugar, salt, and onion seeds. Make a well. Add 200ml (7fl oz) lukewarm water, the yogurt, and ghee or butter. Mix with a wooden spoon for five minutes to form a smooth dough. Cover and keep warm for one hour, until doubled in size.

2 Make the filling by mixing together the feta, chilli, and herbs. Preheat the oven to 240°C (475°F/Gas 9) and put three baking sheets in the oven.

3 Divide the dough into six pieces, and roll each one into a circle about 10cm (4in) wide. Split the filling into six portions, and put a portion into the middle of each circle.

4 Pull the edges up around the filling to form a purse shape. Pinch the edges to seal. Turn the dough over and roll out into an oval, taking care not to tear it.

5 Put the naans onto the preheated baking sheets, and bake for 6–7 minutes, or until well puffed. Move to a wire rack.

258

Peshwari naan bread

Ingredients

500g (1lb 2oz) strong white bread flour,
plus extra for dusting
2 tsp dried yeast
1 tsp caster sugar
1 tsp salt
2 tsp black onion (nigella) seeds
100ml (3½fl oz) full-fat plain yogurt
50g (1¾oz) ghee or butter, melted

For the filling
2 tbsp raisins
2 tbsp unsalted shelled pistachios
2 tbsp almonds
2 tbsp desiccated coconut
1 tbsp caster sugar

Special equipment
food processor with blade attachment

1 Mix together the flour, yeast, sugar, salt, and onion seeds. Make a well. Add 200ml (7fl oz) lukewarm water, the yogurt, and ghee or butter. Mix with a wooden spoon for five minutes to form a smooth dough. Cover and keep warm for one hour, until doubled in size.

2 Make the stuffing by whizzing together all the ingredients in the food processor, until finely chopped. Preheat the oven to 240°C (475°F/Gas 9) and place three baking sheets in the oven.

3 Divide the dough into six pieces and roll each one into a circle about 10cm (4in) wide. Split the filling into six portions, and put a portion into the middle of each circle.

4 Pull the edges up around the filling to form a purse shape. Pinch the edges together to seal. Turn the dough over and roll out into an oval, taking care not to tear it.

5 Put the naans on the preheated sheets and bake for 6–7 minutes, or until well puffed. Move to a wire rack.

259

Focaccia

This dimpled Italian flatbread can be flavoured with herbs, cheese, tomatoes, or olives. Make it your own by adding your favourite ingredients to the dough.

Level rating

How long?   20 mins prep,
                 2 hrs rising,
                 25 mins baking

How many?   8

Ingredients

5 tbsp olive oil, reserve 1 tbsp for dipping,
   plus extra for greasing
350g (12oz) strong white bread flour
2 tsp dried yeast
1 tsp salt
sprigs of rosemary
sea salt, for sprinkling

Special equipment

28 x 18cm (11 x 7in) baking tin

1 Lightly oil the baking tin. Sift the flour into a large bowl and stir in the yeast and salt.

2 Make a well in the centre and add 250ml (9fl oz) lukewarm water and the oil. Mix until it forms a smooth dough.

3 Knead on a clean surface for 10 minutes until smooth. Move to a clean bowl, cover with a tea towel, and leave to rise in a warm place for one hour.

4 Press the dough into the tin so it fills all the corners. Cover with cling film. Leave to rise in a warm place for one hour.

5 Use your fingertips to make dimples in the dough. Sprinkle salt and scatter rosemary over the dough.

Drizzle oil

6 Preheat the oven to 200°C (400°F/Gas 6). Bake for 20–25 minutes until golden and crispy.

PACKED WITH FLAVOUR

Grissini sticks

This Italian breadstick is thin and crispy. It's simple to bake and perfect for a party or an afternoon snack.

Level rating

How long? 45 mins prep,
1½ hrs rising,
18 mins baking

How many? 32

Ingredients

2½ tsp dried yeast

425g (15oz) strong white bread flour, plus extra for dusting

1 tbsp caster sugar

2 tsp salt

2 tbsp extra virgin olive oil

45g (1½oz) sesame seeds

1 Sprinkle the yeast over four tablespoons of lukewarm water. Leave for five minutes, stirring once.

2 Put the flour, sugar, and salt in a bowl. Add the yeast and 250ml (9fl oz) lukewarm water.

Super snappy

3 Add the oil and draw the flour into the liquid, mixing to form a soft, slightly sticky dough.

4 Knead the dough on a floured surface for 5–7 minutes until very smooth and elastic.

5 Cover the dough with a damp tea towel and let it rest for about five minutes.

6 Flour your hands and pat the dough into a rectangle on a well floured work surface.

7 Roll the dough out to a 40 x 15cm (16 x 6in) rectangle. Cover it with a damp tea towel. Leave in a warm place for 1–1½ hours, until doubled in size.

8 Preheat the oven to 220°C (425°F/Gas 7). Dust three baking sheets with flour. Brush the dough with water. Sprinkle with sesame seeds.

9 With a sharp knife, cut the dough into 32 strips, each about 1cm (½in) wide.

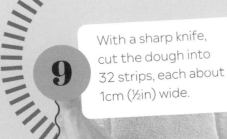

10 Stretch the strips to the width of the baking sheets. Set them on the baking sheets, arranging them 2cm (¾in) apart. Bake for 15–18 minutes. Move to a wire rack to cool completely.

Onion and walnut crown

This delicious bread crown is packed with flavour!
It is ideal for lunch, served with your favourite cheese.

Level rating 🧁🧁

How long?   30 mins prep,
2 hrs 15 mins rising and
proving, 50 mins baking

How many?   1 loaf

Ingredients

2½ tsp dried yeast, dissolved in 4 tbsp
lukewarm milk

425ml (14½fl oz) milk, plus extra for glazing

2 tbsp vegetable oil, plus extra for greasing

2 tsp salt

500g (1lb 2oz) strong white bread flour,
plus extra for dusting

1 large onion, finely chopped

salt and freshly ground black pepper

60g (2oz) walnut pieces

1 Put the dissolved yeast, milk, one tablespoon of the oil, and the salt into a large bowl. Stir in half the flour and mix well with your hand. Add the remaining flour, mix well, and form into a ball. It should be soft and slightly sticky.

2 Knead the dough on a well floured surface for 5–7 minutes, until smooth and elastic. If the dough sticks while kneading, flour the work surface again.

3 Put the dough in a large bowl and cover with a damp tea towel. Leave it to rise in a warm place for 1–1½ hours, until doubled in size.

4 Preheat the oven to 180°C (350°F/Gas 4). Heat the remaining oil in a frying pan. Add the onion, salt, and pepper, and fry for 5–7 minutes, until soft and light brown. Leave to cool.

5 Scatter the walnut pieces on a baking sheet and toast in the oven for 8–10 minutes, until lightly browned. Let the nuts cool, then coarsely chop them.

6 Grease a baking sheet with oil. On a lightly floured work surface, gently knead the dough to knock out the air. Knead the onion and walnuts into the dough until evenly mixed.

7 Shape the dough into a ball. Make a hole in the centre of the ball with two fingers. With your fingers, make the hole bigger, turning to make an even ring, until the ring is 25–30cm (10–12in) in diameter.

8 Put the ring on the baking sheet. Cover with a dry tea towel and leave it to rise in a warm place for 45 minutes, or until doubled in size.

9 Preheat the oven to 200°C (400°F/Gas 6). Brush the ring with milk. Using kitchen scissors, carefully snip around the top of the ring in a zig-zag design.

10 Bake the crown for 45–50 minutes, until well browned. Tap the bottom of the crown with your knuckles; the bread should sound hollow. Move to a wire rack to cool completely.

265

Perfect scones

These tasty scones, served with jam and cream or butter, will really hit the spot! The secret to making successful scones is not to handle the mixture too much or to add too much flour when rolling out the dough.

TRY THIS

For fruit scones, stir in 50g (1¾oz) currants, sultanas, or raisins (or a mixture of these) with the sugar in Step 2 before you add the milk.

Level rating

How long?   10 mins prep,
                12 mins baking

How many?   8–10

Ingredients

50g (1¾oz) unsalted butter, chilled
   and diced, plus extra for greasing
225g (8oz) self-raising flour, plus extra
   for dusting
1 tsp baking powder
pinch of salt
50g (1¾oz) caster sugar
150ml (5fl oz) milk
beaten egg or milk, for brushing

Special equipment
6cm (2½in) pastry cutter

1 Preheat the oven to 220°C (425°F/Gas 7). Lightly grease a large baking sheet with some butter. Sift the flour, baking powder, and salt into a large mixing bowl.

2 Using your fingertips, rub the butter into the flour mixture until it looks like breadcrumbs. Stir in the sugar with a wooden spoon and mix well.

3 Stir in the milk with a round-bladed knife to form a soft dough. Gently knead the dough on a floured surface to remove any cracks.

4 Roll out the dough to 2cm (¾in) thickness, then use the pastry cutter to cut into 8–10 circles. Gather up any trimmings, re-roll them, and cut out more scones.

5 Put the scones on the baking sheet, spacing them a little apart. Using a basting brush, brush the tops with the egg or milk and bake for 10–12 minutes, or until risen and golden brown.

6 Move the scones to a wire rack. Cut them in half and spread with butter and jam, or with whipped cream and jam.

Cornbread

This tasty traditional American bread is super quick to make and goes well with soups and stews.

Level rating

How long?   20 mins prep,
25 mins baking

How many?   8

Ingredients

60g (2oz) unsalted butter, melted and cooled, plus extra for greasing

2 fresh corn cobs, about 200g (7oz) weight of kernels

150g (5½oz) fine yellow cornmeal or polenta

125g (4½oz) strong white bread flour

50g (1¾oz) caster sugar

1 tbsp baking powder

1 tsp salt

2 eggs

250ml (9fl oz) milk

Special equipment

23cm (9in) flameproof cast-iron frying pan or similar-sized loose-bottomed round cake tin

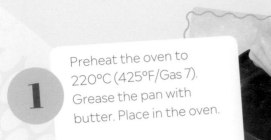

1 Preheat the oven to 220°C (425°F/Gas 7). Grease the pan with butter. Place in the oven.

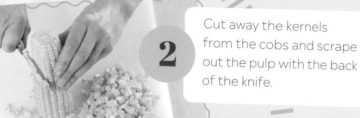

2 Cut away the kernels from the cobs and scrape out the pulp with the back of the knife.

3 Sift the polenta, flour, sugar, baking powder, and salt into a bowl. Add the corn.

4 In a small bowl, whisk together the eggs, melted butter, and milk.

5 Pour three-quarters of the milk mixture into the flour mixture and stir.

6 Draw in the dry ingredients, adding the remaining milk mixture. Stir until smooth.

7 Carefully take the hot pan out of the oven and pour in the batter; it should sizzle.

8 Quickly brush the top with butter. Bake for 20–25 minutes.

9 A skewer will come out clean when the bread is fully baked. Cool slightly on a wire rack before serving.

Top tip

Serve warm, with soup, chilli con carne, or fried chicken. The cornbread does not keep well but leftovers can be used as a stuffing for roast poultry.

Cinnamon rolls

These sweet rolls are packed with flavour. If you want to bake in time for breakfast, leave the rolls to prove overnight in the fridge (after Step 11).

Level rating

How long? 40 mins prep, 4 hrs rising and proving, 30 mins baking

How many? 10–12

Ingredients

125ml (4fl oz) milk

100g (3½oz) unsalted butter, plus extra for greasing

2 tsp dried yeast

50g (1¾oz) caster sugar

550g (1¼lb) plain flour, sifted, plus extra for dusting

1 tsp salt

1 egg, plus 2 egg yolks

vegetable oil, for greasing

For the filling and glaze

3 tbsp ground cinnamon

100g (3½oz) soft light brown sugar

25g (scant 1oz) unsalted butter, melted

1 egg, lightly beaten

4 tbsp caster sugar

Special equipment

30cm (12in) round springform cake tin

1 In a pan, heat 125ml (4fl oz) water, the milk, and butter until just melted. Let it cool to just warm. Whisk in the yeast and a tablespoon of the sugar. Cover for 10 minutes.

2 Put the flour, salt, and remaining sugar in a large bowl. Make a well in the centre and pour in the warm milk mixture.

3 In a small bowl, whisk the egg and yolks, then add to the mixture. Combine to form a rough dough.

4 Put on a floured surface and knead for 10 minutes. Add extra flour if it is too sticky.

5 Put in an oiled bowl, cover with cling film, and keep in a warm place for two hours until well risen.

6 Prepare the filling by mixing two tablespoons of the cinnamon with the brown sugar.

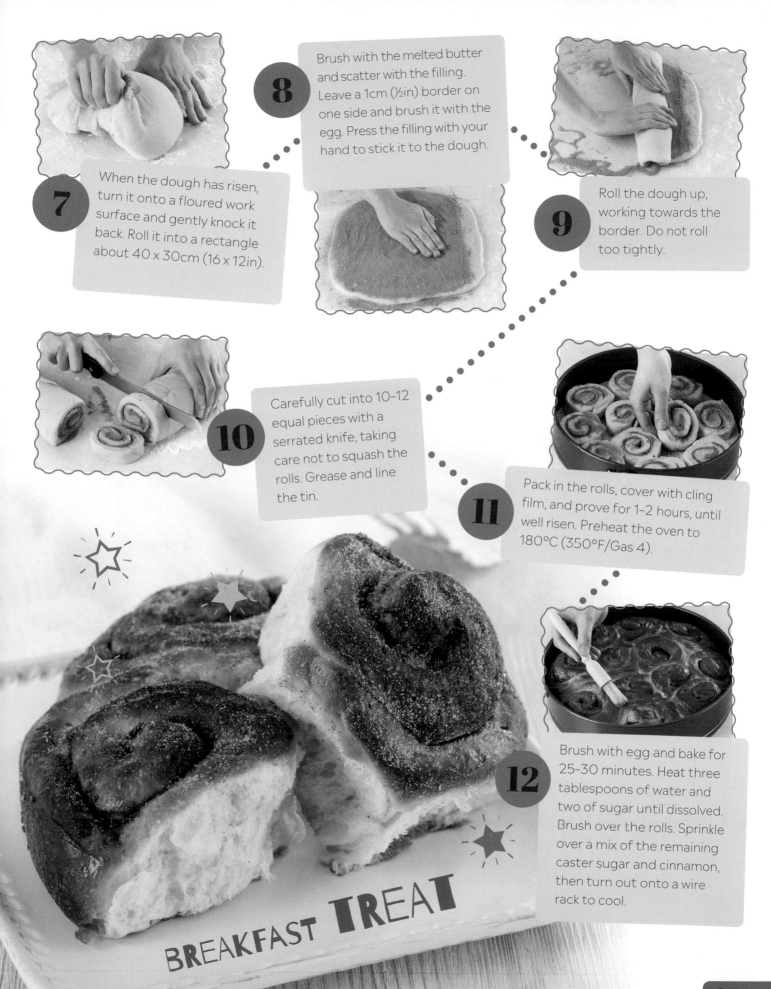

7 When the dough has risen, turn it onto a floured work surface and gently knock it back. Roll it into a rectangle about 40 x 30cm (16 x 12in).

8 Brush with the melted butter and scatter with the filling. Leave a 1cm (½in) border on one side and brush it with the egg. Press the filling with your hand to stick it to the dough.

9 Roll the dough up, working towards the border. Do not roll too tightly.

10 Carefully cut into 10–12 equal pieces with a serrated knife, taking care not to squash the rolls. Grease and line the tin.

11 Pack in the rolls, cover with cling film, and prove for 1–2 hours, until well risen. Preheat the oven to 180°C (350°F/Gas 4).

12 Brush with egg and bake for 25–30 minutes. Heat three tablespoons of water and two of sugar until dissolved. Brush over the rolls. Sprinkle over a mix of the remaining caster sugar and cinnamon, then turn out onto a wire rack to cool.

BREAKFAST **TREAT**

Sticky fruit buns

Honey makes these sweet, fruity buns extra sticky! Traditional fruit buns are made with mixed spice, but you can leave this out if you prefer.

Level rating

How long?   25 mins prep,
                2 hrs 10 mins rising,
                30 mins baking

How many?   10

Ingredients

350g (12oz) strong white bread flour, plus extra for dusting

7g (¼oz) dried yeast

25g (scant 1oz) caster sugar

1 large egg

100g (3½oz) butter, diced, plus extra for greasing

175ml (6fl oz) milk

For the topping

25g (scant 1oz) butter, melted

150g (5½oz) mixture of raisins, currants, and sultanas

25g (scant 1oz) chopped mixed peel

50g (1¾oz) soft light brown sugar

1 tsp ground mixed spice (optional)

grated zest of 1 lemon

1 tbsp clear honey

Special equipment

23cm (9in) round, shallow cake tin

1 Put the flour, yeast, and caster sugar in a large mixing bowl. Make a well in the centre and crack the egg into the well.

2 Melt the butter in a saucepan over a low heat, then add the milk and warm through. Add this to the large bowl and bring together with a round-bladed knife.

3 Turn the dough onto a lightly floured surface and knead for 10 minutes. Return to the bowl, cover with a clean, damp tea towel and leave in a warm place for 1½ hours.

4 Grease the base and sides of the tin and line the base with baking parchment. Preheat the oven to 200°C (400°F/Gas 6).

5 Knock back the dough, then tip it out onto a floured surface. Roll the dough out to a 30cm (14in) square. Brush the melted butter all over it, using a basting brush.

6 Mix together the dried fruit, mixed peel, sugar, mixed spice (if using), and lemon zest. Sprinkle on the pastry, leaving a 1cm (½in) border. Gently roll up the dough into a sausage shape.

7 Use a sharp knife to carefully cut the dough into 10 pieces. Put them in the tin with their cut sides face up. Cover them with a clean damp tea towel and leave in a warm place for 35–40 minutes.

8 Bake for 25–30 minutes, until golden. If they start to become too brown, cover them with foil.

9 Carefully brush the buns with the honey, taking care not to burn yourself on the hot tin. Leave the buns to cool in the tin for 3–4 minutes. Then tip them out onto a wire rack.

FABULOUS AND **FRUITY**

Brioche des rois

Meaning, the "brioche of kings", in French, this bread is traditionally eaten at Epiphany, 6th January. A trinket can be hidden inside to represent the gifts of the Three Kings.

Level rating

How long?   25 mins prep,
6 hrs rising
and proving,
30 mins baking

How many?   10–12

Ingredients

2½ tsp dried yeast

2 tbsp caster sugar

5 eggs, beaten

375g (13oz) strong white bread flour, plus extra for dusting

1½ tsp salt

vegetable oil, for greasing

175g (6oz) unsalted butter, cubed and softened

For the topping

1 egg, lightly beaten

50g (1¾oz) mixed candied fruit (orange and lemon zest, glacé cherries, and angelica), chopped

25g (scant 1oz) coarse sugar crystals (optional)

Special equipment

porcelain or metal *fève* figurine trinket (optional)

25cm (10in) ring mould (optional)

ramekin

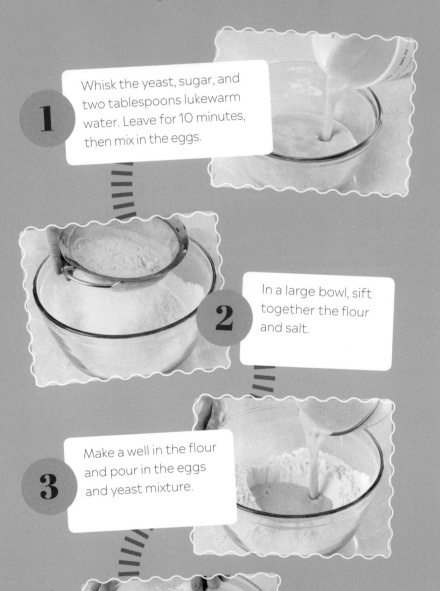

1 Whisk the yeast, sugar, and two tablespoons lukewarm water. Leave for 10 minutes, then mix in the eggs.

2 In a large bowl, sift together the flour and salt.

3 Make a well in the flour and pour in the eggs and yeast mixture.

4 Use a fork and then your hands to bring everything together and form a sticky dough. Turn out the dough onto a lightly floured work surface.

5 Knead the dough for 10 minutes until elastic but still sticky. Put it in an oiled bowl and cover with cling film. Leave to rise in a warm place for 2–3 hours.

6 Transfer to a lightly floured surface and gently knock back the dough.

7 Put one-third of the butter on the dough. Fold the dough over the butter and knead gently for five minutes. Repeat until all the butter is used up. Keep kneading until no streaks of butter show.

8 Form into a round and work it into a ring. Bury the *fève*, if using. Lightly oil a baking sheet and transfer the ring to the sheet or ring mould (if using).

Top tip

This bread will keep in an airtight container for up to three days.

9 Use a ramekin to keep the shape of the hole. Cover with cling film and a tea towel. Leave to prove for 2–3 hours in a warm place, until doubled in size. Preheat the oven to 200°C (400°F/Gas 6).

10 Brush the brioche with beaten egg. Sprinkle over candied fruit and sugar crystals (if using). Bake for 25–30 minutes until golden brown. Leave to cool slightly, then carefully turn out onto a wire rack.

Hefezopf

This traditional sweet German bread is similar to brioche. Its simple plait is easier than it looks to achieve. It can be eaten on its own or with butter.

Level rating

How long? 20 mins prep,
4½ hrs rising
and proving,
35 mins baking

How many? 1 loaf

Ingredients

2 tsp dried yeast

125ml (4fl oz) lukewarm milk

1 large egg

450g (1lb) plain flour,
plus extra for dusting

75g (2½oz) caster sugar

¼ tsp fine salt

75g (2½oz) unsalted butter, melted

vegetable oil, for greasing

1 egg, beaten, for glazing

1 Dissolve the yeast in the warm milk in a small bowl. Let it cool, then add the egg and beat well. In a large bowl, combine the flour, sugar, and salt. Make a well and pour in the milk mixture.

2 Add the melted butter and gradually draw in the flour, stirring to form a soft dough.

3 Knead for 10 minutes on a floured surface until smooth. Put the dough in an oiled bowl and cover with cling film. Keep in a warm place for 2–2½ hours, until doubled in size.

4 Put the dough on a floured work surface and gently knock it back. Divide into three equal pieces.

5 Take each piece of dough and use your palm to roll it into a fat log shape. Continue to roll it towards each end, until it is about 30cm (12in) long.

6 Pinch the tops of the three pieces together and tuck the join under to start the plait. Loosely plait the dough, leaving room for it to rise. Pinch and tuck the ends underneath.

7 Line a baking sheet with baking parchment and place the plait on the sheet. Cover with oiled cling film and a tea towel. Leave in a warm place for two hours; it will not double in size now, but will rise on baking.

8 Preheat the oven to 190°C (375°F/Gas 5). Brush the plait with beaten egg. Bake for 25–30 minutes, until golden. Check if undercooked where the plaits meet.

9 If undercooked, cover with foil and bake for another five minutes. Cool for 15 minutes before serving.

Wrap in **CLING FILM** to keep for up to **TWO DAYS**.

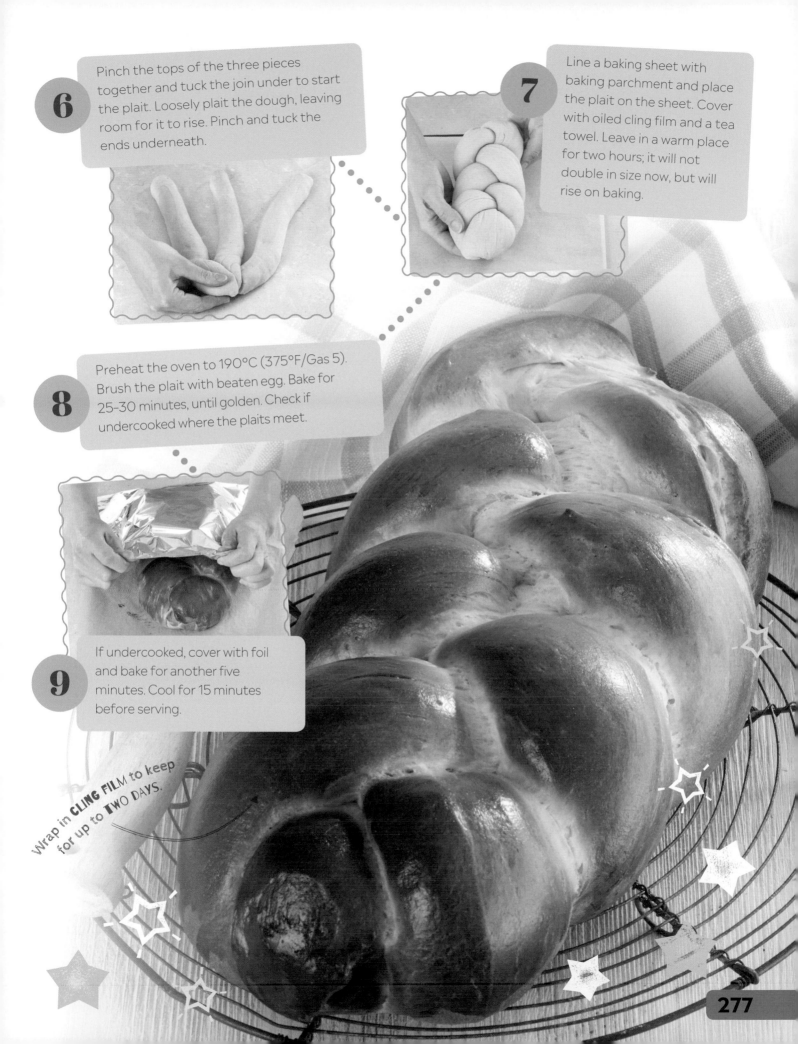

Yule bread

This bread is a delicious festive treat. It needs to be baked a month before it's eaten, so that it can fully moisten and allow time for the flavours to blend.

Level rating

How long?   45 mins prep,
3 hrs rising and proving,
50 mins baking

How many?   1 loaf

Ingredients

1 English breakfast tea bag

90g (3oz) sultanas

90g (3oz) currants

45g (1½oz) dried apricots, chopped

45g (1½oz) candied orange peel, chopped

530g (1lb 3oz) unbleached strong white flour, plus extra for dusting

½ tsp ground cinnamon

½ tsp ground cloves

3 tbsp granulated sugar

1 tsp salt

2 eggs

2½ tsp dried yeast, dissolved in 4 tbsp lukewarm water

125g (4½oz) unsalted butter, softened and cubed, plus extra for greasing

2 tbsp fine brown sugar crystals, to glaze

Special equipment

450g (1lb) loaf tin

1 Soak the teabag in 300ml (½ pint) of boiling water for five minutes. Remove the teabag. Put the dried fruit in a bowl. Pour the tea over the fruit. Let the fruit soak in the tea for 15 minutes. Strain the fruit and reserve the tea.

2 In a large bowl, sift the flour, cinnamon, and cloves. Mix in the sugar, salt, reserved tea, eggs, and yeast. Use your hands to form it into a smooth dough.

3 On a floured surface, knead the dough for 5-7 minutes. Form it into a ball and put in a greased bowl. Cover with a tea towel and let it rise in a warm place for 1–1½ hours, until doubled in size.

4 On a lightly floured surface knead the dough. Let it rest for five minutes. Knead in the butter for five minutes. Cover and let it rest for five more minutes. Knead the soaked fruit into the dough.

5 Cover and rest for five minutes. Grease the tin. Pat the dough into a rectangle 25 x 20cm (10 x 8in). Starting with a long side, roll the rectangle into a cylinder.

6 Roll the cylinder, stretching it until it is about 45cm (18in) long. With the cylinder seam-side up, fold the ends over to meet, making it the length of the tin. Put it in the tin, cover with a tea towel, and let it rise in a warm place for 45 minutes.

7 Preheat the oven to 200°C (400°F/Gas 6) Brush the top of the loaf with water and sprinkle over the sugar crystals.

8 Bake for 15 minutes. Reduce the oven temperature to 180°C (350°F/Gas 4) and bake for a further 45-50 minutes. Remove from the tin and move to a wire rack to cool.

Top tip

To store the loaf, wrap it in baking parchment, then in foil, and keep it in an airtight container for a month before eating.

Panettone

This sweet bread is eaten throughout Italy at Christmas. Making one is not as hard as you might expect and the results are delicious.

Level rating

How long?   30 mins prep,
4 hrs rising and proving,
45 mins baking

How many?   8

Ingredients

2 tsp dried yeast

125ml (4fl oz) milk, warmed in a pan
    and left to cool to lukewarm

75g (2½oz) unsalted butter, melted

2 large eggs, plus 1 small egg,
    beaten, for brushing

1½ tsp vanilla extract

50g (1¾oz) caster sugar

425g (15oz) strong white bread flour,
    plus extra for dusting

large pinch of salt

175g (6oz) mixed dried fruit, such as apricots,
    cranberries, sultanas, and mixed peel

finely grated zest of 1 orange

vegetable oil, for greasing

icing sugar, for dusting

Special equipment

15cm (6in) round springform cake tin
    or high-sided panettone tin

1 In a jug, add the yeast to the warm milk and leave for five minutes. Once the yeast mix is frothy, whisk in the butter, large eggs, and vanilla. In a large bowl, mix the sugar, flour, and salt.

2 Mix the liquid and dry ingredients to form a soft dough; it will be stickier than bread dough.

3 On a lightly floured surface, knead the dough for 10 minutes, until elastic. Form the dough into a loose ball.

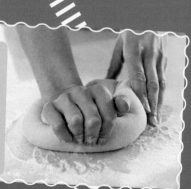

4 Stretch the dough out flat onto a floured work surface. Scatter the dried fruit and orange zest on top and knead again until well combined.

5 Form the dough into a loose ball and put it in a lightly oiled bowl. Cover the bowl with a damp tea towel and leave to prove in a warm place for up to two hours, until doubled in size.

6 Line the tin with a double layer of baking parchment. If using a cake tin, form a collar with the paper, 5–10cm (2–4in) higher than the tin.

7 Knock back the dough with your fist and turn out onto a lightly floured surface.

8 Knead the dough into a round ball just big enough to fit into the tin.

9 Put it into the tin, cover, and leave to prove in a warm place for another two hours, until doubled in size. Preheat the oven to 190°C (375°F/Gas 5).

10 Brush the top of the dough with the small egg. Bake for 40–45 minutes. If it is browning too fast, cover with foil. Leave to cool for five minutes, then turn out. Remove the parchment and cool.

Top tip
Dust with icing sugar before serving.

NO-BAKES

No need to turn on the oven for these tasty treats. Simply crumble, melt, and stir your ingredients to make tealime snacks and perfect puddings. Then pop them in the fridge until you're ready to tuck in.

No bake cool cookies

Not all cookies need to be baked in the oven. These chewy cookies are so easy to make and use only a few simple ingredients. The peanut and chocolate flavour is really rich.

Level rating

How long? 20 mins prep, 30 mins chilling

How many? 12–14

Ingredients

200ml (7fl oz) condensed milk

25g (scant 1oz) butter

2 tbsp light soft brown sugar

50g (1¾oz) crunchy peanut butter

150g (5½oz) porridge oats

125g (4½oz) dark chocolate chips

For the filling

125g (4½oz) cream cheese

2 tbsp crunchy peanut butter

2 tbsp icing sugar

1 Line two baking trays with baking parchment. Put the milk, butter, sugar, and peanut butter in a saucepan over a low heat. Stir until the sugar has dissolved and the butter has melted.

2 Take off the heat and stir in the oats until well combined. Let the mixture cool slightly, then stir in the chocolate chips.

3 Put rounded teaspoons of mixture on the baking trays and flatten slightly. Chill for 30 minutes, until set.

CREAMY AND DREAMY

4

Put the cream cheese, peanut butter, and icing sugar in a bowl and beat with a wooden spoon until smooth and creamy.

5

Spread a little of the filling on the flat side of a cookie, then sandwich together with another cookie. Repeat with the other cookies.

Top tip
The cookies will keep in an airtight container for up to two to three days.

Chocolatey fridge squares

These crunchy chocolate, fruit, and nut squares couldn't be easier to make – they don't even need baking!

Level rating

How long?   15 mins prep,
2 hrs chilling

How many?   18

Ingredients

200g (7oz) dark chocolate (70 per cent cocoa), broken into pieces

100g (3½oz) butter, diced

4 tbsp golden syrup

225g (8oz) digestive biscuits, broken into pieces

125g (4oz) unsalted shelled pistachios

200g (7oz) dried apricots, roughly chopped

100g (3½oz) dried cranberries or cherries

Special equipment

18 x 28cm (7 x 11in) tin

1 Line the base of the tin with baking parchment. Place the chocolate, butter, and golden syrup in a saucepan over a low heat. Stir occasionally until they are melted and smooth.

2 Place all the remaining ingredients in a large mixing bowl and mix well. Pour over the chocolate mixture and stir until all the ingredients are evenly coated.

3 Tip the mixture into the prepared tin and spread it out evenly with the back of a spoon. Chill for at least two hours, or until firm to the touch.

4 Run a blunt knife around the edge of the tin. Carefully turn out onto a chopping board and remove the baking parchment. Cut the fridge cake into 18 squares and serve.

NUTTY AND CHEWY

TRY THIS

You can replace the dried cranberries or cherries with the same quantity of currants, raisins, glacé cherries, or prunes.

Three ways
with fridge cake

Try out these easy "no bake" bars from around the world. Rocky Road was made in the US, Nanaimo came from a town in Canada, and Tiffin was invented in Scotland.

Level rating

How long?
30 mins prep,
2 hrs chilling (Nanaimo
and Rocky Road),
1 hr chilling (Tiffin)

How many?
16 (Nanaimo and Rocky Road)
25 (Tiffin)

Nanaimo

Ingredients

Biscuit layer
115g (4oz) unsalted butter
30g (1oz) cocoa powder
60g (2oz) caster sugar
1 large egg, beaten
200g (7oz) crushed biscuits of choice
75g (2½oz) sliced almonds
50g (1¾oz) unsweetened
  desiccated coconut

Vanilla layer
50g (1¾oz) unsalted butter, softened
300g (10oz) icing sugar
2 tbsp custard powder
½ tsp vanilla extract
2–3 tbsp milk

Chocolate layer
150g (5½oz) dark chocolate, broken
  into pieces
25g (scant 1oz) unsalted butter

Special equipment
20cm (8in) square baking tin, greased
  and lined with baking parchment

The **CHOCOLATE** will **RIPPLE** on top.

1 Melt the butter in a saucepan and mix in the cocoa powder and sugar. Cook for two minutes, whisking continuously.

2 Reduce the heat and whisk in the egg. Cook for 1–2 minutes until it has thickened. Remove from the heat.

3 In a large bowl, mix the biscuits, almonds, and coconut. Pour in the melted cocoa mixture. Combine well and transfer to the tin. Press the mixture down to make an even, firm layer. Chill for 30 minutes.

4 For the vanilla layer, whisk the butter until fluffy. Add the icing sugar, custard powder, vanilla, and milk. Whisk until smooth. Pour it over the base and chill for a further 30 minutes.

5 For the chocolate layer, melt the chocolate and butter in a heatproof bowl over a pan of simmering water. Cool to room temperature. Spread evenly over the vanilla layer. Chill for one hour.

6 Remove from the tin and slice into 16 even-sized pieces.

Rocky Road

Ingredients

250g (9oz) dark chocolate, broken into pieces
100g (3½oz) unsalted butter
2 tbsp golden syrup
150g (5½oz) pretzel sticks, roughly chopped
100g (3½oz) mini marshmallows
50g (1¾oz) unsalted almonds, roughly chopped
50g (1¾oz) dried cherries, roughly chopped

Special equipment
20cm (8in) square baking tin, greased and lined
with baking parchment

TRY THIS
Instead of dried cherries
you can try out raisins
or dried apricots in the
Rocky Road.

1 Melt the chocolate, butter, and golden syrup in a large heatproof bowl over a pan of simmering water. Cool to room temperature.

2 Add the pretzel sticks, mini marshmallows, almonds, and cherries to the chocolate mixture. Stir well until combined.

3 In the tin, spread the mixture out to a firm and even layer. Chill for at least two hours. Remove from the tin and slice into 16 even-sized pieces.

Tiffin

Ingredients

150g (5½oz) unsalted butter
125g (4½oz) golden syrup
45g (1½oz) cocoa powder
300g (10oz) digestive biscuits, crushed
150g (5½oz) dried fruit
250g (9oz) milk chocolate, broken into pieces

Special equipment
20cm (8in) square baking tin, greased
and lined with baking parchment

1 Melt the butter, golden syrup, and cocoa in a saucepan over a low heat, whisking constantly until smooth.

2 Combine the digestive biscuits and dried fruit in a large bowl. Pour over the butter mixture and mix together.

3 Tip the mixture into the tin and spread it out to a firm, even layer. Chill for at least 30 minutes.

4 Melt the chocolate in a heatproof bowl over a saucepan of simmering water. Cool to room temperature. Spread it over the biscuit base. Chill for 30 minutes.

5 Take out of the tin and slice into 25 even-sized pieces.

Top tip
All of these "no bake" bars can be stored in an airtight container for up to five days.

289

Tasty tiramisu

This Italian treat is a light, layered dessert of coffee-flavoured sponge fingers and mascarpone that will melt in your mouth!

Level rating

How long?   30 mins prep, 6 hrs chilling

How many?   8

Ingredients

2 tbsp instant decaf espresso powder
120ml (4fl oz) almond syrup

For the filling

6 large egg yolks
135g (5oz) icing sugar, sifted
85ml (2¾fl oz) vanilla syrup
450g (1lb) mascarpone cheese, at
   room temperature
500ml (16fl oz) double cream, chilled
400g (14oz) sponge fingers
unsweetened cocoa powder,
   for dusting

Special equipment

33 x 23 x 5cm (13 x 9 x 2in) tin or dish

1 Measure out 500ml (16fl oz) boiled water and let it cool for five minutes. Mix the water with the espresso powder and almond syrup in a bowl. Set aside. For the filling, whisk the egg yolks and icing sugar in a heatproof bowl for 2–3 minutes, until thick and pale in colour.

2 Place the bowl over a saucepan of simmering water, making sure it does not touch the water. Add the vanilla syrup whisking constantly to combine. Whisk the mixture for five minutes, until thick and ribbon-like in texture. Remove from the heat, cover, and cool.

3 Place the mascarpone in a large bowl and fold gently with a spatula to soften the cheese. Then add the cooled egg yolk and syrup mixture. Whisk gently until well combined and smooth.

4 In a separate bowl, whisk the double cream to form stiff peaks. Fold a little of the cream into the mascarpone mixture and mix well. Then gently fold in the rest and mix until it is well combined.

5 Dip half of the sponge fingers into the coffee mixture, briefly on each side, and use them to line the bottom of the serving dish. Cover with half of the cream filling and sift some cocoa powder on top.

6 Add another layer of sponge fingers and filling. Sprinkle generously with cocoa powder, wrap in cling film, and chill for 4–6 hours. Remove the tiramisu from the fridge 15 minutes before serving.

No-bake lemon cheesecake

This zesty cold-set cheesecake doesn't need to be baked, making it lighter and fluffier than a baked cheesecake.

Level rating

How long? 30 mins prep, 4½ hrs or overnight chilling

How many? 8

Ingredients

250g (9oz) digestive biscuits
100g (3½oz) unsalted butter, diced
4 gelatine sheets, roughly cut up
finely grated zest and juice of 2 lemons
350g (12oz) cream cheese
200g (7oz) caster sugar
300ml (10fl oz) double cream
pared lemon zest, to decorate

Special equipment

23cm (9in) round springform cake tin

1 Line the base of the tin with baking parchment. Put the biscuits in a bag and crush with a rolling pin to crumbs.

2 Melt the butter and pour it over the crushed biscuits, mixing well to combine.

3 Press the biscuit mixture firmly into the base of the tin using a wooden spoon. Chill for 30 minutes.

4 In a small heatproof bowl, soak the gelatine in the lemon juice for five minutes to soften.

5 Place the bowl over a pan of hot water and stir until the gelatine melts. Set aside to cool.

6 Beat together the cream cheese, caster sugar, and lemon zest until smooth.

7 In a separate bowl, whisk the double cream to form soft peaks. Make sure it is not stiff.

8 Beat the gelatine mixture into the cream cheese mixture, stirring well to combine.

9 Gently fold the whisked cream into the cheese mixture. Be careful not to lose any volume.

10 Tip the cheese mixture onto the chilled biscuit base and spread evenly.

11 Smooth the top with a damp palette knife or the back of a damp spoon.

12 Chill for at least four hours or overnight. Run a sharp, thin knife around the inside of the tin.

13 Gently turn out the cheesecake onto a serving plate. Sprinkle the pared zest over the top. Remove the baking parchment before slicing.

Top tip

The cheesecake can be made up to two days ahead and stored in the fridge.

No-bake lime and blueberry cheesecake

This fruity cheesecake is packed with sweet blueberries and zingy limes, giving it a mouthwateringly good flavour. Make sure you measure the gelatine carefully to perfectly set the filling.

Level rating

How long?   30 mins prep,
                  6½ hrs chilling or overnight

How many?   8

Ingredients

250g (9oz) digestive biscuits,
  finely crushed
100g (3½oz) unsalted butter, melted

For the topping

100g (3½oz) blueberries
1 tbsp caster sugar
grated zest of ½ lime

For the filling

juice of 2 limes
12g (¼oz) powdered gelatine
300g (10oz) soured cream
100g (3½oz) caster sugar
500g (1lb 2oz) full-fat cream cheese
grated zest of 1 lime, plus extra to serve
1 tsp vanilla extract

Special equipment

23cm (9in) springform cake tin

1 Line the base of the tin with baking parchment. Combine the biscuit crumbs and butter in a bowl. Spread the mixture in the base of the tin, pressing down firmly. Chill for 30 minutes.

2 For the topping, gently heat the blueberries, sugar, zest, and one tablespoon of water in a saucepan. Stir until the blueberries release their juices. Remove from the heat. Leave to cool.

3 For the filling, whisk the lime juice and gelatine in a saucepan. Leave for five minutes. Then heat gently, whisking, until the gelatine dissolves. Let it cool. In a bowl, whisk the cream, sugar, cream cheese, zest, and vanilla, then whisk in the gelatine mix. Spread the filling evenly over the biscuit base.

4 Spoon over the topping and decorate with the juices. Chill for 4–6 hours, or overnight. Take out of the tin and sprinkle with lime zest to serve.

Show it off

Once you've baked something special you might want to show it off on social media, especially if it's the first time you've mastered a baking technique. Here are some tips on how to present and photograph anything from delicious pastries, pies or bread to impressive celebration cakes.

You will need

- tiered cake stand, plate, bowl, tray, wire cooling rack, wooden board, basket
- tablecloth, napkin, tea towel, oven gloves
- mixed crockery, small serving plates and bowls
- cutlery, cake forks, spoons, knives, cake slice
- drinks (tea, hot chocolate, milk, juice)
- cups, mugs, teacups, glasses
- extra ingredients from a recipe (berries, sprinkles, cocoa powder, icing sugar, herbs, nuts, edible flowers), small sieve or flour shaker
- coloured paper and card or mini bunting, wooden kebab sticks, gift bags, balloons, scissors, glue

1 Set the scene for your baked item. Would it be eaten at breakfast? If so, create a simple breakfast table setting. If you've made a showstopper cake for a party then think about where it will sit. Could it be the centrepiece on a buffet table?

Top tip

Think about the timing. Does your baked item need to be shot straight away, before it shrinks in size or melts? Does it need to be kept in the fridge until you're ready to whip it out to take a pic?

2 Select the right dish to present your baked item on. Would a cake stand, plate, bowl, tray, wire rack, wooden board, or basket suit your baked item? A tiered cake stand would be best for cupcakes, whereas a basket would be perfect for bread.

3 Think about what the surface material should be. Would a tablecloth, patterned napkin, tea towel, or oven gloves add to the scene? Always choose simple patterns so you don't take the focus away from the food.

4 Choose the right crockery to be in the background of a shot, such as a pile of dessert plates or bowls. If it's a party scene then perhaps paper plates or napkins in a stack would suit the scene.

5 Do you need any drinks in the background? Would a cup of tea, mug of hot chocolate, glass of milk or juice add to the shot? Make sure you select a drink that would go with the baked item you've made.

6 Would it help to have cutlery, such as a sharp knife, cake fork, or cake slice to accompany your baked item? Try to keep it simple and don't choose something that will take the attention away from the cake or other bake.

7 Sprinkling a few extra ingredients around from your bake can add to your photo. Use a small sieve to shake icing sugar or cocoa powder over a bake. You can also drop on edible glitter, sugar strands, or cake confetti. Scattered berries, edible flowers, nuts, and chocolate shavings can also add to the shot.

8 Adding in decorative elements, such as bunting, gift bags, balloons, and presents can really help add to your photo. However, don't let the party bits and pieces take over the shot.

Snap and share

Taking a decent photo of food doesn't just happen by luck, you need to think about lighting, orientation, colour, focus, shadows, angles, and backgrounds. These are skills you can easily learn when you're setting up something to snap on your camera or phone.

TRY THIS

Flick through this book to get ideas. Which shots of the finished baked goods inspire you? Follow cookery bloggers or vloggers. Read a few cookery magazines that specialize in baking.

Think about...

Colour
Make sure the surface colour works for the food you're photographing. See pages 296–297 for advice on choosing props. Don't let strong patterns on a tablecloth take attention away from the food.

Shadows
If you take a photo outside then do so on a cloudy day. Bright sunshine casts strong shadows. A cloudy sky is better as the light is more even.

Lighting
Natural daylight is ideal for taking photos of food. Artificial light can wash out the image and make the food look unappealing. Shoot inside and near a window.

Angle
Try out different angles. You can photograph your food overhead, straight on, or from an angle, looking slightly down or tilted up.

Orientation
Decide if a photo taken landscape or portrait would suit your finished bake. For example, a tiered cake stand is tall, so might be better taken as a portrait shot. These pretzels work well as a landscape image.

Focus
Choose where you want your focal point to be. A lot of mobile phones and tablets allow you to click and pinpoint exactly where you want the camera to focus.

Background
Clear any clutter away, unless you want a messy shot of all the aftermath of baking a cake. Neutral wallpaper or a lightly painted wall both work well as backgrounds.

Overhead

This focaccia bread looks great when photographed overhead. The oil and balsamic vinegar dip also add to the set-up of this final shot. It's irresistible!

Variations

Think about getting lots of variations. Always take a photo of the whole cake, for example, before you cut out a slice.

Less is more

Remember it's the food you're trying to show off, so don't over-style or prop your picture. This impressive chocolate roulade has been placed on a white dish and plain tablecloth, to show off the food, not the props.

Adding in extras

Photograph a cake on its own, before adding in extras to create a different look. Place a relevant item from the recipe, such as this cut and partially peeled orange. Don't overdo it though.

How many?

Consider how many bakes you want to photograph. If you've made a batch of muffins, do you want one muffin in the foreground and the rest on a wire rack in the background?

Share it

Once you've taken the the perfect picture, share it with your family and friends. They'll probably want the recipe too.

Glossary

This is the place to find extra information about the baking terms and techniques used in this book.

A, B

alternate doing two things in turns, such as adding an egg, then some sugar, then adding another egg.

baking blind weighing down a pastry base with baking beans or foil to stop it from rising during baking.

batch making or baking things in more than one go, usually if you do not have enough tins or space in the oven.

batter a thin, liquidy dough that is used to make light cakes, pancakes, and to coat food before it's fried.

beat stirring or mixing quickly until smooth, using a whisk, spoon, or mixer.

blend mixing ingredients together in a blender or food processor until combined.

boil heating liquid in a pan over a high temperature so that it bubbles strongly.

C

chill cooling food in a fridge.

choux soft pastry that is piped onto a tray instead of being rolled out. The dough bakes to form crisp, hollow balls that are then filled.

coarse food that is in small pieces.

combine mixing ingredients together evenly.

compote fruit cooked in syrup.

consistency how runny or thick a mixture is.

cream beating butter and sugar together to add air.

crème pâtissière a creamy custard used as a filling.

crimp shaping something into small ridges, or folds.

crumb coat thin layer of icing applied to a cake to trap the crumbs, before a final layer of icing is applied.

curdle when the liquid and solid parts of an ingredient or mixture separate. Milk curdles when over-heated and cake mixtures can curdle if the eggs are too cold or added too quickly.

D

dice cutting an ingredient into small, equal cubes.

dissolve melting or liquifying a substance (often sugar in water).

dough the mixture of flour, water, sugar, salt and yeast (and possibly other ingredients) before it is baked into bread.

drain removing excess liquid by pouring ingredients through a colander, or by resting on kitchen paper.

drizzle pouring slowly, in a trickle.

E, F, G, H

elastic a mixture with a stretchy texture.

filo tissue-thin sheets of pastry. Best bought, as making it from scratch is incredibly difficult.

fine incredibly small, often powdery pieces of food that have been ground down from a larger portion.

fold mixing ingredients together gently, to keep as much air in the mixture as possible.

fondant a thick icing that is rolled out, cut, and shaped into decorations for cakes, cupcakes, and pastries.

frangipane a paste made from almond-flavoured cream, used as a filling.

frosting a topping that is usually a creamy icing.

fry cooking food in oil.

ganache a filling made from chocolate and cream.

glaze coating food in a liquid to give it a smooth, glossy surface.

grate shredding an ingredient into little pieces by rubbing it against a grater.

grease rubbing butter or oil onto a baking sheet, tin, or tray to stop food from sticking.

hollow something that is empty inside. Bread sounds hollow when cooked.

I, J, K

incorporate blending together.

individual a single one, or enough for one person.

juice squeezing liquid out of a fruit or vegetable.

knead pressing and folding dough with your hands until it is smooth and stretchy. This distributes the yeast and helps it to rise.

knock back deflating risen dough with a gentle punch. This evens out the texture of the bread.

L, M, N, O

level making the surface of something the same height.

line placing baking parchment or foil in a tin so that food won't stick to it.

lukewarm mildly warm.

macaron a small, round dessert made from two halves with a cream filling.

mash crushing ingredients with a fork or masher.

melt heating a solid substance until it becomes a liquid.

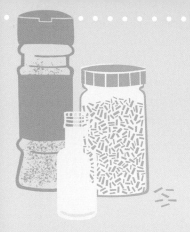

meringue a light and airy dessert that's made from beaten egg whites and sugar, and baked until crisp.

mix combining ingredients together, either by hand or with equipment.

moist something which is slightly wet.

no bake a sweet dish that is chilled in a fridge instead of baked in an oven.

overwork if food is handled, beaten, or rolled out too many times then it doesn't work as well in a recipe.

P, Q, R

palmier a sweet pastry that's made in the shape of a palm leaf.

pastry a sweet or savoury baked item made from flour, fat, and water.

pasty a small pie made with pastry that folds around vegetables, meat, or cheese.

pavlova a dessert made with a meringue base and filled with cream and fresh fruit.

peaks raised areas that look like the tops of mountains.

pie a baked pastry (savoury or sweet) that usually has an outer case and a top.

pipe making a strip of icing as a decoration on a cake or cupcake. Meringues are also piped from a piping bag.

portion an amount or helping of food.

preheat turning the oven on and heating it to the correct temperature before baking food in it.

process blending an ingredient or ingredients in a food processor.

proving the final rise of bread dough before baking.

pulp squishing food so that it's crushed, wet, and soft.

quantity how much of an ingredient you need.

rest putting pastry in a cool place.

rich strongly flavoured.

ripe when a fruit is soft and ready to be eaten.

rise dough gets bigger in size when left in a warm place.

roll out flattening out and shaping dough or pastry using a rolling pin.

rub in rubbing flour and butter together with your fingers to create a texture that looks like breadcrumbs.

S

sandwich sticking two sides or halves together, usually with a mixture in between.

savoury something that does not taste sweet.

score making shallow cuts across the surface of a baked food.

season adding salt, pepper, vinegar, or other spices to a dish to add flavour.

serrated the pointy, tooth-like edge of a knife.

set leaving food on the work surface, in the fridge, or in the freezer until it firms up and turns solid.

shortcrust pastry a crisp and crumbly pastry that's used for tarts, flans, and pies.

sift using a sieve to remove lumps from dry ingredients.

simmer cooking over a low heat, so the liquid or food is bubbling gently but not boiling.

skewer a metal or wooden stick with a sharp end.

slice using a knife to cut food into strips.

sprinkle scattering a food lightly over another food.

stone removing the stone from fruit or vegetables.

streusel a crumbly filling or topping that is often flavoured with cinnamon.

T, U, V

tart a pastry case that has a savoury or a sweet filling.

tepid mildly warm.

texture the way something feels, e.g. soft, smooth, chunky, or moist.

tiers layers of cake stacked on top of each other.

transfer moving something from one place to another.

traybake a sweet food that is made in a square or rectangular tin.

trimmings leftover pieces of dough or pastry from cutting out.

turn out taking out of a pan or tray and carefully laying on a surface used for serving.

volume, adding increasing the size of a mixture, such as when whisking egg whites.

W, X, Y, Z

well a dip made in flour, in which to crack an egg or pour liquid into.

whisk evenly mixing ingredients together with a whisk.

yeast a type of fungus that, when added to flour, water, sugar, and salt, causes the mixture to rise.

zest the skin of a citrus fruit that has been grated with a grater or a zester.

Index

Acknowledgements

DORLING KINDERSLEY would like to thank the following people for their assistance in the preparation of this book: Dave King for photography, Anne Damerell for legal assistance, Laura Nickoll for proofreading, Eleanor Bates, Rachael Hare, Charlotte Milner, and Claire Patane for design assistance, Helen Peters for compiling the index, Anne Harnan for recipe testing, and Becky Walsh for hand modelling.

The publisher would like to thank the following for their kind permission to reproduce their photographs: (Key: a-above; b-below/bottom; c-centre; f-far; l-left; r-right; t-top)
9 123RF.com: Lilyana Vynogradova (c). Dreamstime.com: Ra3rn (cla). 258 Dreamstime.com: Maglara (bl). 278 Dreamstime.com: Roberts Resnais (cla). 296 123RF.com: Belchonock (bl). 297 123RF.com: Serezniy (cra) Cover images: Front: Alamy Stock Photo: Tim Gainey; Back: Alamy Stock Photo: Tim Gainey

The publisher would also like to thank the following for their work on the original recipes that are re-used in this book:

The Cook's Book (ISBN 9781405303378)
Introduction: Jill Norman; Flavorings: Peter Gordon; Stocks & Soups/Poultry & Game Birds/Fruit & Nuts: Shaun Hill; Chinese Cooking: Ken Hom; Breads & Batters: Dan Lepard; Eggs & Dairy Produce/Pasta & Dumplings: Michael Romano; Fish & Shellfish/Vegetables: Charlie Trotter. Senior Project editors: Annelise Evans, Michael Fullalove, Pippa Rubinstein, Consulting editor Norma MacMillan, Senior Art editors: Susan Downing, with Alison Donovan, Editors: Lucy Heaver, Caroline Reed, Frank Ritter, Designer Alison Shackleton, Art director Carole Ash, Publishing director Mary-Clare Jerram, Publishing manager Gillian Roberts, DTP designer Sonia Charbonnier, Production controller Joanna Bull, Photographers: Steve Baxter, Martin Brigdale, Francesco Guillamet, Jeff Kauck, David Munns, William Reavell. Hugh Thompson, for his initial planning and management of the project. Bridget Sargeson, food stylist, for her unfailing professionalism and good humour in preparing and presenting for the camera over half of the techniques and recipes in this book. All of the chefs who generously made available their facilities and materials for photography. Editorial assistance Valerie Barrett, Shannon Beatty, Stuart Cooper, Roz Denny, Barbara Dixon, Anna Fischel, Kay Halsey, Karola Handwerker, Eleanor Holme, Katie John, Bridget Jones, Jenny Lane, Beverly le Blanc, Irene Lyford, Marie-Pierre Moine, Constance Novis, Gary Werner, Fiona Wild, Jeni Wright. Design assistance Maggie Aldred, Briony Chappell, Murdo Culver, Jo Grey, Toni Kay, Elly King, Luis Peral-Aranda, Judith Robertson, Liz Sephton, Penny Stock, Sue Storey, Ann Thompson. DTP design assistance Alistair Richardson, Louise Waller. Editorial consultation Rosie Adams, Henja Schneider, Margaret Thomason, Jill van Cleave, Kate Whiteman, Jennifer Williams. Index Dawn Butcher, Chefs' liaison Marc Cuspinera Viñas (for Ferran Adrià), Jennifer Fite (for Rick Bayless); Marion Franz (for Stephan Franz); Rosie Gayler (for Paul Gayler); Barbara Maher (for Stephan Franz); Anna Elena Pedron (for Norman Van Aken); Anne Roche-Nöel (for Pierre Hermé); Lucy Rushbrooke (for Greg Malouf); Rochelle Smith (for Charlie Trotter); Elisabeth Takeuchi (for Hisayueki Takeuchi); Jane Wareing (for Marcus Wareing); David Whitehouse (for Dan Lepard). On behalf of the contributing chefs the following chefs prepared and styled food and demonstrated cooking techniques for photography: Sébastien Bauer (for Pierre Hermé), Jeffrey Brana (for Norman Van Aken), Marc Cuspinera Viñas (for Ferran Adrià), Julien Tessier (for David Thompson), Guiseppe Tentori (for Charlie Trotter). Food stylists Stephana Bottom, Angela Nilsen, Lucinda Rushbrooke (for Greg Malouf), Nicole Szabason, Linda Tubby, Kirsten West (for Rick Bayless), Sari Zernich (for Charlie Trotter). Susanna Tee for recipe testing. Hand models Virpi Davies, Harriet Eastwood, Saliha Fellache, Caroline Green, Jane Hornby, Olivia King, Emma McIntosh, Carlyn van Niekerk, Brittany Williams, Bethan Woodyatt, Tanongsak Yordwai (for David Thompson). Props stylists Victoria Allen, John Bentham, Bette Blau, Andrea Kuhn, Hendrik Schaulin, Helen Trent. Photographic studio production Carol Myers and Alex Grant at Divine Studio/Piquant Productions, New York; Sid Kelly at Code Management Inc., Miami; Oliver Beuvre-Méry at Blanc Loft, Gentilly, Paris; Nicole Werth and Stefan Richter at Lightclub, Photographic, Hamburg. Administrative assistance, Laura Dixon, Alex Farrell, Zoe Moore, Jolyon Rubinstein.

The Children's Baking Book (ISBN 9781405341431)
Recipes and Styling by Denise Smart, Photography by Howard Shooter, Project Editor Heather Scott, Senior Designer Lisa Sodeau, Editor Julia March, Home Economist Denise Smart, Managing Editor Catherine Saunders, Art Director Lisa Lanzarini, Publishing Manager Simon Beecroft, Category Publisher Alex Allan, Production Controller Nick Seston, Senior Production Editor Clare McLean, and US Editor Margaret Parrish.

The Illustrated Step by Step Cook (ISBN 9781405357180)
Editor Lucy Bannell, Project Editor Sarah Ruddick, US Editor John Searcy, Managing Editor Dawn Henderson, Managing Art Editors Christine Keilty, Marianne Markham, Senior Jacket Creative Nicola Powling, Senior Presentations Creative Caroline de Souza, Category Publisher Mary-Clare Jerram, Art Director Peter Luff, Production Editor Maria Elia, Production Controller Alice Holloway, Creative Technical Support Sonia Charbonnier, DK INDIA: Designer Devika Dwarkadas, Senior Editors Rukmini Kumar Chawla, Saloni Talwar Design Manager Romi Chakraborty, DTP Designers Dheeraj Arora, Manish Chandra, Nand Kishore, Arjinder Singh, Jagtar Singh, Pushpak Tyagi, DTP Manager Sunil Sharma, Production Manager Pankaj Sharma Photographers: David Murray, William Reavell, William Shaw, Jon Whitaker, Prop stylist: Liz Belton, Food stylists: Lizzie Harris, Sal Henley, Cara Hobday, Jane Lawrie, Phil Mundy, Jenny White, Art directors: Nicky Collings, Anne Fisher, Luis Peral, Indexer: Hilary Bird, Proofreader: Irene Lyford, Americanizers: Jenny Siklos, Rebecca Warren, and US consultant: Kara Zuaro

Illustrated Step-by-Step Baking (ISBN 9780756686796)
Author Caroline Bretherton Senior Editor Alastair Laing, Project Art Editor Kathryn Wilding, US Editor Rebecca Warren, Managing Editor Dawn Henderson, Managing Art Editor Christine Keilty, Senior Jacket Creative Nicola Powling, Senior Production Editor Maria Elia, Senior Production Controller Alice Holloway, Creative Technical Support Sonia Charbonnier, Photographers Howard Shooter, Michael Hart DK INDIA: Project Editor Charis Bhagianathan, Senior Art Editor, Neha Ahuja, Project Designer Divya PR, Assistant Art Editor Mansi Nagdev, Managing Editor Glenda Fernandes, Managing Art Editor Navidita Thapa, DTP Manager Sunil Sharma, Production, Manager Pankaj Sharma, DTP Operators Neeraj Bhatia, Sourabh Challariya, Arjinder Singh, Art Directors: Nicky Collings, Miranda Harvey, Luis Peral, Lisa Pettibone, Props Stylist Wei Tang, Food Stylists: Kate Blinman, Lauren Owen, Denise Smart, Home Economist Assistant Emily Jonzen, Baking equipment used in the step-by-step photography kindly donated by Lakeland, www.lakeland.co.uk, Caroline de Souza for art direction and setting the style of the videos and presentation stills photography, Dorothy Kikon for editorial assistance and Anamica Roy for design assistance, Jane Ellis for proofreading and Susan Bosanko for indexing. Thanks to the following people for their work on the US edition: Consultant Kate Curnes, Americanizers: Nichole Morford and Jenny Siklós, and Steve Crozier for retouching.

A Little Course in Baking (ISBN 9781409365211)
Senior Editor Alastair Laing, Project Art Editor Gemma Fletcher, Managing Editor Penny Warren, Managing Art Editor Alison Donovan, Senior Jacket Creative Nicola Powling, Jacket Design Assistant Rosie Levine, Pre-production Producer Sarah Isle, Producer Jen Lockwood, Art Directors Peter Luff, Jane Bull, Publisher Mary Ling, DK Publishing, North American Consultant Kate Curnes, Editor Margaret Parrish, Senior Editor Rebecca Warren, DK INDIA: Senior Editor Garima Sharma, Senior Art Editor Ivy Roy, Managing Editor Alka Thakur Hazarika, Deputy Managing Art Editor Priyabrata Roy Chowdhury, Tall Tree Ltd: Editor Emma Marriott, Designer Ben Ruocco, Written by Amanda Wright, Design assistance Jessica Bentall, Vicky Read, Editorial assistance: Helen Fewster, Holly Kyte, DK Images: Claire Bowers, Freddie Marriage, Emma Shepherd, Romaine Werblow, Indexer Chris Bernstein DK DELHI: Assistant Art Editor Karan Chaudhary, Art Editor Devan Das, Design assistance Ranjita Bhattacharji, Simran Kaur, Anchal Kaushal, Prashant Kumar, Tanya Mehrotra, Ankita Mukherjee, Anamica Roy, Editors: Kokila Manchanda, Arani Sinha, DTP Designers: Rajesh Singh Adhikari, Sourabh Chhallaria, Arjinder Singh, CTS/DTP Manager Sunil Sharma.

Step-by-Step Cake Decorating (ISBN 9781409334811)
Author Karen Sullivan, DK UK: Project Editor Martha Burley, Project Art Editor Kathryn Wilding, Managing Editor Dawn Henderson, Managing Art Editor Christine Keilty, Producer, Pre-Production Sarah Isle, Producers: David Appleyard, Jen Scothern, Art Director Peter Luff, Publisher Peggy Vance, Cake Decorators Asma Hassan, Sandra Monger, Amelia Nutting, DK US: US Senior Editor Rebecca Warren, US Editor Margaret Parrish, North American Consultant Kate Ramos, DK INDIA: Senior Editor Charis Bhagianathan, Senior Art Editors: Ira Sharma, Balwant Singh, Editor Janashree Singha, Assistant Art Editors: Tanya Mehrotra, Aastha Tiwari, Managing Editor Alicia Ingty, Managing Art Editor Navidita Thapa, Production Manager Pankaj Sharma, Pre-Production Manager Sunil Sharma, Senior DTP Designer Jagtar Singh, DTP Designers: Satish Chandra Gaur, Rajdeep Singh, Rajesh Singh, Sachin Singh, Anurag Trivedi, Manish Upreti.

Kids' Birthday Cakes Step by Step (ISBN 9781409357193)
Author Karen Sullivan, Project Editor Kathy Woolley, Designer Harriet Yeomans, Managing Editor Dawn Henderson, Managing Art Editor Christine Keilty, Pre-Production Senior Producer, Tony Phipps, Senior Producer Jen Scothern, Art Director Peter Luff, Publisher Peggy Vance, US Consultant Kate Curnes Ramos, US Editor Jenny Siklos, US Senior Editor Margaret Parrish, Cake Decorators Sandra Monger, Hannah Wiltshire, Kasey Clarke, Juniper Cakery, DK INDIA: Project Editor Bushra Ahmed, Senior Art Editor Ira Sharma, Editor Ligi John, Art Editor Simran Kaur, Assistant Art Editor Sourabh Challariya, Managing Editor Alicia Ingty, Managing Art Editor Navidita Thapa, Pre-Production Manager Sunil Sharma, DTP Designers Rajdeep Singh, Manish Upreti, Mohammad Usman.

Step-by-Step Desserts (ISBN 9780241189092)
Authors: Caroline Bretherton, Kristan Raines, DK LONDON: Project Editor Martha Burley, Senior Art Editor Sara Robin, Project Art Editor Vicky Read, Editorial Assistant Alice Kewellhampton, Design Assistant Laura Buscemi, Managing Editor Dawn Henderson, Managing Art Editor Christine Keilty, Senior Jacket Creative Nicola Powling, Pre-Production Manager Dragana Puvacic, Senior Producer Stephanie McConnell, Creative Technical Support Sonia Charbonnier, Deputy Art Director Maxine Pedliham, Publisher Peggy Vance, DK US: US Editor Christy Lusiak, US Senior Editor Margaret Parrish, US Consultant Kate Ramos, DK INDIA Senior Art Editor Ira Sharma, Editors: Neha Samuel, Seetha Natesh, Art Editors: Zaurin Thoidingjam, Tashi Topgyal Laya, Deputy Managing Editor Bushra Ahmed, Managing Art Editor Navidita Thapa, Pre-production Manager Sunil Sharma, DTP Designer Rajdeep Singh.

Eat Your Greens (ISBN 9780241250228)
Senior Designer Sadie Thomas, Editors: James Mitchem, Carrie Love, US Editor Margaret Parrish, Editorial assistant Sopia Danielsson-Waters, Art direction for photography Charlotte Bull, Photographer Dave King, Food Stylist Georgie Besterman, Nutritional Consultant Fiona Hunter, Recipe Consultant Lorna Rhodes, US Consultant Kate Ramos, Senior Producer Leila Green, Pre-Production Producer Dragana Puvacic, Creative Technical Support Sonia Charbonnier, Managing Editor Penny Smith, Managing Art Editor Mabel Chan, Publisher Mary Ling, Art Director Jane Bull, Proofreader Caryn Jenner, Photoshoot Assistance: Eleanor Bates, Rachael Hare, Charlotte Milner, Illustrator Sadie Thomas, Picture Library Assistance: Lucy Claxton, Laura Evans. Models: Barney Allen, Lindsay Guzman, Egypt Hanson, Rio Lewis, Grace Merchant, Liberty Moore, and Olivia Phokou.

Cooking Step by Step (ISBN 9780241300374)
Senior Editor James Mitchem, Senior Designer Elaine Hewson, Art Direction for Photography Charlotte Bull, Designers: Charlotte Bull, Samantha Richiardi, Editorial Assistance Sally Beets, Carrie Love, Photographer Dave King, Home Economist and Food Stylist Denise Smart, Recipe Tester Sue Davie, Pre-Production Controller Tony Phipps, Senior Producer John Casey, Creative Technical Support Sonia Charbonnier, Managing Editor Penny Smith, Managing Art Editor Mabel Chan, Publisher Mary Ling, Art Director Jane Bull, James Tye for additional photography, Marie Lorimer for indexing, Eleanor Bates, Lynne Murray, Sakshi Saluja, and Romaine Werblow for picture library assistance, and Rachael Hare, Violet Peto, and Artie King for help during the photoshoots.